The Wit and
Wisdom of Shakespeare

The Wit and Wisdom of Shakespeare

32 Sonnets Made Thoroughly Accessible

Darrel Walters

ROWMAN & LITTLEFIELD
Lanham • Boulder • New York • London

Published by Rowman & Littlefield
A wholly owned subsidiary of The Rowman & Littlefield Publishing Group, Inc.
4501 Forbes Boulevard, Suite 200, Lanham, Maryland 20706
www.rowman.com

Unit A, Whitacre Mews, 26-34 Stannery Street, London SE11 4AB, United
Kingdom

British Library Cataloguing in Publication Information Available

Library of Congress Cataloging-in-Publication Data

Library of Congress Cataloging-in-Publication Data Available ISBN 978-1-
4758-1835-2 (cloth : alk.
paper) ISBN 978-1-4758-1836-9 (pbk. : alk. paper) — ISBN 978-1-4758-
1837-6 (electronic)

∞^{TM} The paper used in this publication meets the minimum requirements
of American National Standard for Information Sciences—Permanence of
Paper for Printed Library Materials, ANSI/NISO Z39.48-1992.

Printed in the United States of America

Contents

Foreword

Had William Shakespeare never written a play, he would nonetheless be revered by today's readers for the remarkable body of non-dramatic poetry he produced. Indeed, this poetry might be better known if its myriad delights did not suffer at least a partial eclipse in the shadow of his brilliant plays. The purpose of this immensely helpful volume is to introduce the contemporary reader to the abiding pleasures of Shakespeare's sonnets.

The sonnets include some of the finest poems of love and friendship ever written. But for all of their splendors, Shakespeare's sonnets can be hard to read, particularly for twenty-first-century readers. Both language and literary conventions have changed drastically. This admirable edition is designed to make their pleasures available to a wide contemporary audience. Nothing would have pleased Shakespeare more, since throughout the sonnets, he is concerned about his future readership; indeed, he even makes the success of his commemorative endeavors depend on the poems' being read in the future. "Not marble nor the gilded monuments/ Of princes shall outlive this powerful rhyme," declares Sonnet 55 proudly. But the rhyme is only powerful if it is read. And that power is in our hands. This book is designed to help us keep up our end of the bargain.

Even experienced readers sometimes need help with Shakespeare's language and syntax, which are made more difficult by time and shifting literary taste. Readers in particular need help with the sonnet form. There is in the shape of a sonnet a productive tension between form and content: the emotions described are invariably messy, but sonnets are

a tightly controlled form. This edition will help today's reader appreciate the remarkable formal virtuosity that Shakespeare achieves in the
astonishing space of fourteen lines; it will also help the reader glimpse
the amazing range of human experience Shakespeare is able to convey
in this comparatively constricted form. The sonnet becomes in Shakespeare's skillful hands a little "thinking machine," capable of articulat-
ing over fourteen lines a stunning range of attitudes and experiences.

Shakespeare's friend and fellow dramatist Ben Jonson suggested
that Shakespeare was "not of an age, but for all time." This has proved
prophetic: the sonnets are indeed relevant to anyone whose intimate
relationships include the gamut of comfort and despair, faith and betrayal, hope and fear. Jonson also suggests that although dead, Shakespeare is "alive still, while thy book doth live,/ And we have wits to
read, and praise to give." Shakespeare worried as much as any writer
about whether his work would continue to be read in the future; indeed,
he made that hope the bulwark against the inevitable decay of time.
Although he invests great power in writing, then, it is a fragile power,
which is contingent on his work continuing to be read. In reading these
poems afresh, as this commendable edition helps us do, we assist at the
performance of what Sonnet 65 describes as a "miracle," that somehow
these poems will continue to reach across the centuries and ensure that
"in black ink my love may still shine bright." Every time we read these
poems, we experience the privilege, and the pleasure, of making this
miracle occur anew.

Michael Schoenfeldt
John Knott Professor of English Literature
Former Chair, Department of English Language and Literature
University of Michigan

Preface

William Shakespeare! His name is both respected and feared among young students of English literature, and his writing seems to intimidate as many readers as it enlightens. While we're told by good authority that he's the best of the best, we find his plays and poetry difficult to penetrate—a room full of treasure behind a locked door. Inside that room are jewels of wit, wisdom, and insight—bedecked with golden language—with many a potential reader barred from entry by unusual words and words used in unusual ways. At the root of the problem are differences in time and culture, along with the mysterious workings of Shakespeare's remarkably fertile mind.

How can we get ourselves into that room? A sensible point of entry might be Shakespeare's shortest works: his sonnets. He wrote 154, each a self-contained sample of his genius and style, and each encompassing only fourteen lines. The selected sonnets enclosed here, made thoroughly accessible by this book's unique design, might serve as a doorway into other works of Shakespeare. But then, *The Sonnets* are much more than that. They are amazing little packages of enlightenment wrapped in beautiful language—well worth understanding and enjoying for themselves.

Whether you are a student trying to understand Shakespeare's work or someone simply wanting to explore the richness of this grand body of literature, *The Wit and Wisdom of Shakespeare* will help you find your way to understanding, appreciation, and delight. The accompanying video recordings, in which the author recites each sonnet contained in the book, will enhance your appreciation even further.

Though only a fraction of Shakespeare's 154 sonnets are presented here, they will take you deep enough into the collection to orient you well. Your experience with these 32, as prepared for this book, will help you read, understand, and appreciate others of the remaining 122 sonnets—and the writings of Shakespeare in general.

Darrel Walters
Ambler, Pennsylvania
Professor Emeritus, Temple University

Acknowledgments

This book would not have been written without the encouragement and assistance of my friends Bob Sheppard and Geoffrey Thomas. Their tireless help in reading and commenting on manuscripts and their assistance in recording sonnet recitations were invaluable. Various degrees of reading or work with the recordings also came from Jean Arfield, Jennifer Bubser, Roger Dean, Kerry Green, Thea Howey, Ejner Jensen, Michael Schoenfeldt, Johanna Walters, Walter Weidenbacher, Emily Abram and her fellow English teachers at Wissahickon High School, and Temple University recording engineer David Pasbrig.

Scott Rowland tirelessly recorded and edited the final, on-site versions of the sonnet recitations, and Stephen Schreiber played the harpsichord accompaniments. Appreciation for sites used is due Byer's Choice, Ltd., Fairmount Park Horticultural Center, Amy Scarlett at Gwyn Meadows Farm, Morris Arboretum of the University of Pennsylvania, Presbyterian Church of Chestnut Hill, Rick Pool, St. Thomas Church Whitemarsh, Stony Creek Homeowners Association, Stotesbury Estates, Wissahickon Valley Park, and Meg and Frank Kolachny, who lent their son Jacob to the recording of Sonnet #2.

The late Marcella O'Connor, a high school English teacher from Muskegon, Michigan, has played a greater role in my writing than anyone can know. The force of her will and the power of her lessons continue to light my path many decades later. I can never thank this model teacher adequately.

Above all, I am indebted to my wife, Carol, whose years of forbearance, help, and advice have woven threads through all that I do. Her constant love and support are a part of this book in ways unique to her.

WILLIAM SHAKESPEARE
1564–1616

The words of Sonnet 74 (p. 36) ring loudly this 400th year after Shakespeare was "carried away" by "that fell arrest without all bail." Was he urging only the recipient of the sonnet to "be contented" after his passing, or was he speaking to all of us—to all posterity—when he said

> The earth can have but earth, which is his due.
> My spirit is thine, the better part of me.

Though we swell with admiration at representations of his physical being in various sketches, paintings, and statues, Shakespeare himself—through his poetry and plays—has confirmed the view that he gave of his own physical worth in the couplet of Sonnet 74:

> The worth of that is that which it contains,
> And that is this, and this with thee remains.

How enormously thankful we are that the content of Shakespeare's spirit does indeed "with us remain" four centuries after his passing. And how particularly thankful we are for *The Sonnets*, in which the breadth and depth of his spirit and his reservoir of personal thoughts are exposed most fully.

CHAPTER 1

The Sonnets of William Shakespeare

The meat of this book is in chapters 2 through 6. That's where the sonnets themselves are presented and described. This chapter contains background and perspective on *The Sonnets*, a description of sonnet format, an overview of this book's organization, and a few suggestions for its use. To absorb what this chapter has to say is to be rewarded with a greater understanding and fuller enjoyment of everything that follows.

BACKGROUND AND PERSPECTIVE

Although background information about Shakespeare's sonnets is abundant, it's also sketchy and conflicting. Edward Hubler says, in "Shakespeare's Sonnets and the Commentators,"

> With the possible exception of Hamlet, no work of Shakespeare's has called forth more commentary and controversy than his sonnets, and on no other work has more nonsense been written. There is, indeed, ample reason for diversity of opinion. We do not know when the sonnets were written, to whom they were addressed, or if they are autobiographical at all. (1962, 3)

So the background is a quagmire. Because this book is aimed at understanding and appreciating *The Sonnets* as delightful works of art, not at trying to untangle their convoluted history, the background given here will be skeletal. If you're interested in an extensive account of all the intrigue behind *The Sonnets*, you'll want to consult other sources.

Many scholars believe, but are not certain, that Shakespeare wrote some sonnets to a young man (Sonnets 1–126) and others to a beguiling and frustrating woman (Sonnets 127–154). The identity of each of those persons is unknown. The young man in question is likely to have been not only a friend, but a nobleman and a potential patron whose favor Shakespeare was pursuing.

The woman to whom some of the sonnets are supposed to have been written is frequently referred to as the dark lady. That label ostensibly refers to the darkness of her beauty at the beginning of their relationship and the darkness of her character and deeds at the end. The specific nature of Shakespeare's relationship with her is unknown.

A third party in the intrigue is sometimes called the rival poet. Even more shadowy than the other figures, he may be accounted for in any one of several ways. He may have been a noted poet of the time with whom Shakespeare competed, or Shakespeare's composite of such poets, or even a pure invention—a prop that Shakespeare created for his art.

Most of the speculation written about Shakespeare and his sonnets over the centuries since they were first published has as much evidence working against it as for it:

- Speculation that *The Sonnets* are autobiographical is weakened by, among other things, knowledge that young Shakespeare at times wrote from the viewpoint of an old man (Sonnets 73 and 74).
- Speculation that each sonnet was written to a specific person solely for private consumption seems at odds with his allusions to posterity as an audience: "so long as men can breathe or eyes can see" (Sonnet 18); "dwell in lovers' eyes" (Sonnet 55). Nor does the personal-poetry theory fit with the broad content of some sonnets, such as Sonnet 116's mission to define love, and Sonnet 66's enumeration of Shakespeare's complaints about the human condition.
- Speculation that sonnets written to the young man are indications of homosexuality is at odds with Shakespeare's urging the young man to marry and have children (Sonnets 1–17), and with the explicit heterosexual characterization of both himself and the young man in Sonnet 20. (Still, nothing is known definitively on this count.)

Disagreement abounds. Scholars argue about when *The Sonnets* were written (most believe mid-1590s) and about whether the sequence, first published by William Thorpe in 1609 (Willen and Reed 1964, v), is Shakespeare's doing. Some even question whether Shakespeare wrote every sonnet contained in the collection. Because the first publication occurred during his lifetime—though likely not with his approval—the sonnets were almost certainly all from his pen. Had they not been, he would hardly have kept quiet about it for the last eight years of his life. Detractors who insist on drumming up lame evidence to the contrary were dealt a blow very cleverly some time ago by George Kittredge, of Harvard, who "at a banquet honoring Shakespeare, proved by means of clever anagrams that Francis Bacon had written the menu" (Giroux 1982, 14).

Disagreements about the nature of Shakespeare's relationship with the young man are legion. Some characterize it as homosexual. Others see it solely as one of respect and fondness—not to mention good business. At the root of the controversy are Shakespeare's declarations of love, but his language should not be interpreted as it would be today. As Edward Hubler notes in *The Sense of Shakespeare's Sonnets*, "With Shakespeare affection is a universal, and his name for it is love" (1952, 98).

C. L. Barber, in "An Essay on Shakespeare's Sonnets," from Harold Bloom's *Modern Critical Interpretations: William Shakespeare's Sonnets*, offers a parallel observation. He writes that the love Shakespeare expresses to the young man is

> a most important kind of love which is ordinarily part of a relationship but here becomes the whole . . . love by *identification* rather than sexual possession. (1987, 18)

Expressing love in that larger sense was common in Shakespeare's time. We also need to keep in mind that some of the sonnets supposed to have been written to the young man may not have been. Only those having masculine pronouns are certain to have been written to a male recipient.

Besides, there is still uncertainty as to how much of Shakespeare's sonnet writing was directed at anyone in particular, and how much was generic art. Northrop Frye, in "How True a Twain," notes that: "the experience of love and the writing of love poetry do not necessarily have any direct connection. One is experience, the other craftsmanship" (1962, 31).

Shakespeare's intense expression of love in a universal sense gives *The Sonnets* universal appeal and universal application. No matter the identity or gender of a sonnet's supposed recipient, it can be read, enjoyed, and applied as anyone desires it to be, and with wondrous effect.

In the end, probably the issue of Shakespeare's sexual orientation is best left a non-issue. The more conjecture one reads the more one sees that the answer—homosexual, bisexual, or heterosexual—is unknown, and will remain so unless some telltale artifact pops out at us unexpectedly. Rather than wonder about that which is not available to us, we might do well to put our time and attention on enjoying that which is available: the writings themselves.

W. H. Auden echoes Hubler in claiming that "there has been more nonsense written about Shakespeare's *Sonnets* than any other piece of literature extant" (2000, 86). He is particularly critical of attempts to identify characters related to *The Sonnets*:

> It is an idiot's job, pointless and uninteresting. It is just gossip, and gossip, though it can be exceedingly interesting when the parties are alive, is not at all interesting when they're dead. (2000, 86)

Also showing disdain for the perpetuation of nonsense is Patrick Cruttwell in his essay "Shakespeare's Sonnets and the 1590s," in Barbara Herrnstein's *Discussions of Shakespeare's Sonnets*. He attributes the lack of serious critical attention paid to these Shakespeare masterpieces to

> the fatal and futile attraction they have exercised on the noble army of cranks, who are far too busy identifying the young man, the dark lady, the rival poet, and William Shakespeare, to bother about the quality of the poetry. (1964, 46–47)

The Sonnets may be, more than anything, a medium of expression that Shakespeare found engaging for a time, much as a composer might concentrate on string quartets during one period and symphonies during another. If so, that would indicate that many of his sonnets are likely to have been written as freestanding works of art, intended to be read and enjoyed across generations.

The Wit and Wisdom of Shakespeare is written with that generic view in mind, focusing primarily on the pure enjoyment of these gems. If this book does its job, you'll enjoy the extraordinary beauty created when words are used artfully, you'll understand and appreciate *The Sonnets* as a whole, and you'll find personal value within specific sonnets. Many of the world's great poets have found themselves in that company. Hubler (1962, 10–11) reveals a litany of praise for Shakespeare's sonnets as art. Wordsworth says, "There is not a part of the writings of this Poet wherein is found in equal compass a greater number of exquisite feelings felicitously expressed." Keats is said to have read *The Sonnets* with "passionate interest and excitement." And Edward Fitzgerald said that *The Sonnets* showed him who Shakespeare was: "I had but half an idea of him . . . till I read them carefully."

THE SONNET FORMAT

Knowing the underlying design of these sonnets will help you understand and appreciate them. The traditional Elizabethan sonnet, named for its rise during the reign of Britain's Queen Elizabeth I, is written in a rhythm and meter known as *iambic pentameter*. An *iamb* is an unstressed syllable followed by a stressed syllable (a<u>bout</u>). *Iambic pentameter* describes poetry whose lines each contain five iambs (ta-<u>tum</u>, ta-<u>tum</u>, ta-<u>tum</u>, ta-<u>tum</u>, ta-<u>tum</u>).

The Elizabethan sonnet contains fourteen lines written in iambic pentameter. Its rhyme scheme binds the first twelve lines into three four-line sets (quatrains) by alternate-line rhyming The last two lines break that pattern, as they rhyme with each other (a couplet). The couplet is typically indented a bit to call attention to its climactic importance and its variance from the previous pattern of alternate-line rhymes set into quatrains. Here is a schema of the Elizabethan sonnet:

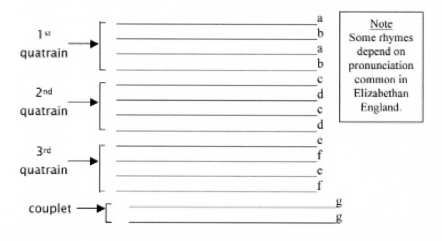

Shakespeare uses this form with poetic license. That is, he sometimes awards himself the freedom to bend parameters for effect. Though iambic pentameter is clearly the rule, sometimes vestiges of iambic pentameter can be found only be eliding over an extra unstressed syllable or by substituting a sliver of silence for a missing syllable. He is more consistent with the rhyme schemes: all but three of his 154 sonnets (Sonnets 126, 153, and 154) contain fourteen lines having the rhyme scheme shown, and nearly all of those 151 are organized into three quatrains and a couplet. Of the thirty-two sonnets contained in this book, all contain fourteen lines and the conventional rhyme scheme, but one—Sonnet 66—is organized without three distinct quatrains.

A fair question to ask is "Why? What is the function of those formal restrictions placed on Elizabethan sonnets?" Intelligent conjecture is found in Michael Schoenfeldt's *The Cambridge Introduction to Shakespeare's Sonnets*: "If the chosen formal constraints of the sonnet are about anything, it is the effort to impose pattern and form on the chaos of existence" (2010, 89). The skillful sonneteer elicits a certain sense of wonder by encasing the chaos of a sonnet's content in the orderliness of its presentation. A reader (or listener) is likely to feel satisfaction in, and admiration for, an author's ability to express "deeply unstable emotions within the formal liturgy of the sonnet" (89). The insight and lucidity apparent in Schoenfeldt's observations suggest that his work is a good place to begin further exploration of *The Sonnets*.

While understanding the sonnet format, its function, and its effect on readers is interesting and important, you will want to put format into the background when you begin to read *The Sonnets*. Appreciation and enjoyment are enhanced by attending to meaning over rhyme and meter. If the sonnet content were simplistic, like a verse written for children, it could be read with regular, lilting rhythms:

A shaggy dog came running like a clown
About the time my mom came out the door.
The grass was wet; he slipped and knocked her down.
The dog was fine, but Mom was bruised and sore.

But such a lilt would be devastating to a Shakespeare sonnet. While rhyme and meter serve the cohesiveness and the beauty of *The Sonnets*, they do so subtly and with flexibility. They need to be bent a bit. For example, read the third quatrain of Sonnet 29 with an ear to meaning:

> Yet in these thoughts myself almost despising,
> Haply I think on thee, and then my state,
> Like to the lark at break of day arising
> From sullen earth, sings hymns at heaven's gate;

You will see (hear) that the strong, regular stress points shown in the child's piece would sound ridiculous. A meaningful reading will have you pause in irregular places and plow through the rhyme at the end of line three. Use this same good-sense judgment in reading all of the sonnets.

THE ORGANIZATION OF THIS BOOK

Chapters two through six are built on five topical categories, created to add cohesion and make each sonnet easier to understand by its common ground with others. The focus of the sonnets by chapters is as follows:

> Chapter 2, "Living Life's Span": a cross-section of life's experiences that encompass young and old.
> Chapter 3, "Seeing the Unseen": feelings so intense that they conjure up images more powerful than those before the eye.
> Chapter 4, "Declaring Devotion": typical Shakespeare love sonnets, expressing devotion far beyond the ordinary.
> Chapter 5, "Managing Relationships": depicting issues of infatuation, competition, apology, mindset, growth, heartbreak, and regret.
> Chapter 6, "Keeping Beauty Alive": Shakespeare's obsession with preserving beauty over time.

Cases could be made for reassigning sonnets from one topical category to another (Sonnet 2 would fit into chapter 6), or for inserting some excluded sonnets into these categories, or for creating other categories altogether. In short, the categories on which the chapters are built have been created arbitrarily as a simple aid to accessibility.

Each sonnet is presented in multiple ways to enhance understanding. First is a presentation of the sonnet itself, followed on the same page by an Essence Statement that characterizes its basic message. Across the page is a Diagram for Greater Understanding—a widely spaced rendition of the sonnet with potentially puzzling words and phrases bracketed and clarified. Last is a two-page Description and Interpretation in simple, straightforward language, expounding on the thoughts that Shakespeare expressed and noting some of the devices he used.

SUGGESTIONS FOR USING THIS BOOK

You can use the series of presentations for a given sonnet in any way you find helpful. One approach is to follow this sequence:

- Read the sonnet through to get a general idea of what is there and identify problems and questions. Use the Essence Statement simultaneously to orient yourself to the whole, but be unconcerned about difficulties you encounter. They will be clarified soon.
- Refer to the Diagram for Greater Understanding to clarify puzzling words and phrases. The sonnet as presented within this diagram is not intended to be read fluently. It amounts to an examination of trees at the expense of the forest.
- Read the Description and Interpretation to broaden your overall understanding of the sonnet. Probably you will refer back to parts of the sonnet periodically.
- Read the sonnet again. Having had obstructions removed and understanding enhanced, you will enjoy it more fully.

After following the sequence above—or another approach if you prefer—read the sonnet you are studying aloud a few times. Schoenfeldt says of reading the sonnets aloud, "only then can the music and the cacophony of a given line be fully apprehended" (2010, 5). You might even memorize a given sonnet if that suits you. Effect an occasional pause or emphasis that helps you deliver the meaning as you understand it to be. If you wish, listen to the recitation of the sonnet provided as an adjunct to this book for another interpretation. You will feel yourself absorb more of the sonnet's meaning and value each time through. C. L. Barber emphasizes the importance of repetition:

> To read and re-read is essential if we are to enjoy the way each moves, the use it makes of the possibilities of the sonnet form, the particular development in it of a design of sounds and images. (1987, 9)

As your relationship with these intriguing little poems by Shakespeare grows, you'll see value beyond anything expressed here. Any number of subtleties could be cited within the descriptions and interpretations presented in this book, and you would still find interesting aspects of particular sonnets that occur only to you. Great literature nourishes individual minds in unique ways. Interpretations given here are not meant to promote a point of view, but rather to offer a catalyst for your personal relationship to *The Sonnets*.

RLm

That time of year thou mayst in me behold
When yellow leaves, or none, or few, do hang
Upon those boughs which shake against the cold,
Bare, ruined choirs where late the sweet birds sang.

—*from Sonnet 73*

CHAPTER 2

Living Life's Span
Sonnets 2, 50, 66, 30, 60, 73, and 74

The sonnets in this chapter, tending as they do toward gloominess, are not prototypical Shakespeare sonnets. They open this book because they encompass a broad sweep of life's experiences. They show that day-to-day heartaches and hopes of people have changed little in 400 years. Through them, Shakespeare illuminates circumstances and thoughts that commonly descend on us throughout the span of life. How do I cope with the loss of my youthful good looks? Why must I be separated from persons important to me? Why do many unjust circumstances contaminate a world that I think should be better and more pure? How do I dare complain about problems, sadness, and suffering I've endured when I have the blessing of your rich friendship? Why does time treat us so well early in life and so poorly later? Will the twilight of my life bring greater devotion from loved ones because of the little time we have left together? Will those I leave behind after death feel that I left something important of myself with them?

These are powerful questions to ponder. They are made even more powerful by Shakespeare's ability to jar us from everyday thought with profound insight and artful language—to pull us into the essence of human existence and dazzle us with brilliant encapsulations of complex issues.

The circumstances brought to light by these sonnets probably have touched the life or passed through the mind of each of us at one time or another, and left a hazy residue at the perimeters of our thought. Shakespeare churns up that residue, breathes life into it, and transports us to a deeper consciousness—one that sets off mental fireworks and leaves us feeling more alive, more in touch with life's struggles, and less alone with our problems.

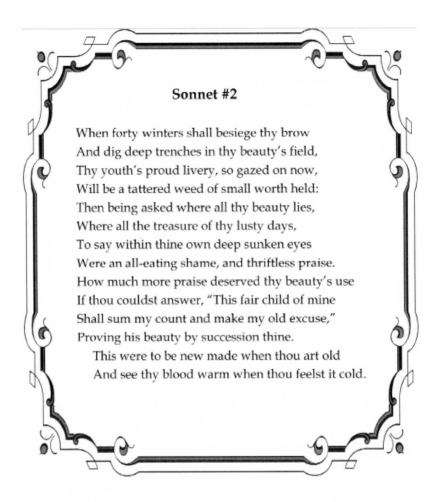

Sonnet #2

When forty winters shall besiege thy brow
And dig deep trenches in thy beauty's field,
Thy youth's proud livery, so gazed on now,
Will be a tattered weed of small worth held:
Then being asked where all thy beauty lies,
Where all the treasure of thy lusty days,
To say within thine own deep sunken eyes
Were an all-eating shame, and thriftless praise.
How much more praise deserved thy beauty's use
If thou couldst answer, "This fair child of mine
Shall sum my count and make my old excuse,"
Proving his beauty by succession thine.
    This were to be new made when thou art old
    And see thy blood warm when thou feelst it cold.

The Essence of Sonnet #2

After time removes your youthful beauty, you will do
well to have a child who testifies to your former self.
When you become old, you will remember this advice.

To fully experience the sonnets visit www.sonnetsofshakespeare.com for a
live recording by Darrel Walters.

Diagram for Greater Understanding

1st Quatrain

forty years of living   attack your features
When [forty winters] shall [besiege thy brow]

carve wrinkles   your lovely face
And [dig deep trenches] in [thy beauty's field,]

appearance
Thy youth's proud [livery,] so gazed on now,

unattractive
Will be [a tattered weed] of small worth held:

2nd Quatrain

Then being asked where all thy beauty lies,

Where all the treasure of thy lusty days,

your beauty is internal
To say [within thine own deep sunken eyes]

insincere
Were an all-eating shame, and [thriftless] praise.

3rd Quatrain

How much more praise deserved thy beauty's use

If thou couldst answer, "This fair child of mine

show what I've accomplished   justify my old age
Shall [sum my count] and [make my old excuse,"]

you passed your good looks on to him
Proving [his beauty by succession thine.]

Couplet

you'll recall this advice
[This were to be new made] when thou art old

(your child)   (you)
And see thy blood [warm] when thou feelst it [cold.]

SONNET 2

Description and Interpretation

The first seventeen of Shakespeare's sonnets are commonly called the "birth sonnets" or "procreation sonnets." He writes to a "beautiful" young man (a term used more commonly then than "handsome"), offering reasons for him to marry and have children. Some scholars speculate that the procreation sonnets were commissioned by the young man's mother, who was fearful that he would not marry and reproduce, and who had been unable to convince him to do so. Further speculation identifies Lady Pembroke as the likely suspect, working on behalf of her son, William Herbert. All that speculation rests on a flimsy bed of what-ifs and guesswork.

The first quatrain of this sonnet looks like a scare tactic. Winter, the harshest of seasons, represents the year, and it "besieges" the brow—sounding like a violent attack. *You're beautiful now, but that's not going to last. Old age* (beyond age forty in those days!) *is out there waiting for you, and what it's going to do to you will not be pretty.* The tattered weed metaphor is consistent with Shakespeare's common practice of using a rose to signify beauty and a weed the opposite. This first quatrain is unusually strong and self-contained. Shakespeare more commonly begins sonnets with a thought that needs development and resolution. These opening lines simply force the reader from the start to confront the reality that each of us, in time, will grow old and lose much of our physical appeal.

In the second and third quatrains, Shakespeare warns that the young man will do himself no favor by rationalizing, as the years pass, that his beauty has become internal. *You will be shorting yourself,* Shakespeare says, *if you forego a praiseworthy use of your beauty.* He tells the young man that his physical beauty is an asset to be exploited—a genetic advantage by which to attract a mate—and raw material from which to produce equally beautiful offspring. He goes into detail about the distinct, tangible rewards awaiting the young man if he were to become a father. *Other people,* he argues, *will see clearly that this beautiful young child is your progeny. It will be almost as if they are seeing you again in your prime. Through this child you will preserve your own physical beauty before it has a chance to wither.*

This preservation-through-procreation theme is common in the early sonnets. In Sonnet 3, for example (not included in this book), Shakespeare points out physical similarities between the young man and his mother as evidence that the young man's offspring will follow suit.

> Thou art thy mother's glass [mirror], and she in thee
> Calls back the lovely April of her prime;
> So thou through windows of thine age shalt see,
> Despite of wrinkles, this thy golden time.

Just as you have preserved your mother's likeness, so can you depend upon your offspring to preserve yours.

Line 11 of this sonnet offers two specific accounts of how fathering a child will reflect well on the young man. "Sum my count" hints that he will be seen to have taken a series of responsible steps in his life, which in turn add up to an impressive sum: the beautiful child. "Make my old excuse" is a way to say that having something to show for the onset of old age will justify what he has lost with time.

One aspect of this sonnet that makes it unusual is that it feels complete at the end of the third quatrain: "Proving his beauty by succession thine." Usually the couplet of an Elizabethan sonnet is more consequential than this one. Readers of sonnets come to expect that the couplet will reveal a large, final thought—one that puts everything into perspective—or that it will be a well-crafted summation of the three preceding quatrains, or perhaps an alternate view that turns back on the rest of the sonnet in a way that produces a "wow" moment. This couplet, in contrast, sounds like an afterthought. It says *when you see that child's robust countenance years from now in contrast to your older self you'll recall this advice vividly, almost as if it were a new revelation.* Though it has some degree of function, the couplet doesn't feel integral to the whole. One wonders if Shakespeare might have finished the first twelve lines thinking, "Woops, I wrapped it up too soon. It feels complete. Oh well, the sonnet form that I'm using does require a closing couplet, so . . ."

We'll never know if these imaginings are anywhere near the truth.

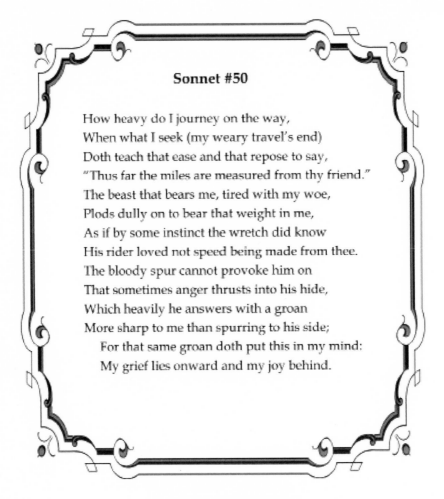

Sonnet #50

How heavy do I journey on the way,
When what I seek (my weary travel's end)
Doth teach that ease and that repose to say,
"Thus far the miles are measured from thy friend."
The beast that bears me, tired with my woe,
Plods dully on to bear that weight in me,
As if by some instinct the wretch did know
His rider loved not speed being made from thee.
The bloody spur cannot provoke him on
That sometimes anger thrusts into his hide,
Which heavily he answers with a groan
More sharp to me than spurring to his side;
    For that same groan doth put this in my mind:
    My grief lies onward and my joy behind.

The Essence of Sonnet #50

I journey with a heavy heart, conscious of the miles
I put between us. Even my horse balks, sensing my
hesitation, and so makes me ever more aware of the
joy I leave behind.

To fully experience the sonnets visit www.sonnetsofshakespeare.com for a live recording by Darrel Walters.

Diagram for Greater Understanding

1ˢᵗ Quatrain

          sadly   **travel away from home**

How [heavy] do I [journey on the way,]

When what I seek (my weary travel's end)

         torment me when I rest

Doth [teach that ease and that repose to say,]

"Thus far the miles are measured from thy friend."

2ⁿᵈ Quatrain

            sensing my unhappiness

The beast that bears me, [tired with my woe,]

         (emotional and physical)

Plods dully on to bear that [weight] in me,

As if by some instinct the wretch did know

        resists making this journey

His rider [loved not speed being made from thee.]

3ʳᵈ Quatrain

(symbol of the rider's frustration)

The [bloody spur] cannot provoke him on

That sometimes anger thrusts into his hide,

Which heavily he answers with a groan

  (stabbing me with sadness)

More [sharp to me] than spurring to his side;

Couplet

For that same groan doth put this in my mind:

you are not where I'm going   **you are where I've been**

[My grief lies onward] and [my joy behind.]

SONNET 50

Description and Interpretation

A common source of confusion in Shakespeare's writing, particularly in his sonnets, is his penchant for attributing human will to inanimate or abstract entities (a practice known as *personification*). Frequently, for example, he makes "Time" a proper noun (see Sonnet 60, p. 28), referring to it as "he" or "him." In Sonnet 128 (p. 94), he says that the keys of a harpsichord are "happy," and that his lips would gladly trade places with those keys—as if both the keys and his lips are willful beings.

In this sonnet, Shakespeare goes a step further by breathing life into two periods of time: the end of a journey and the period of rest that follows. He claims that Journey's End (uppercase is mine) teaches Ease and Repose to victimize him: *When this traveler tries to grab that rest and relaxation that you normally give*, says Journey's End to Rest and Repose, *don't let him get comfortable. Instead, remind him that what he's accomplished with this journey is to put unwanted miles between himself and his friend.*

Shakespeare didn't have to write a sonnet to say what he had to say. He could have just told his friend directly *once I got there I couldn't rest from my trip, because all I could think about was how far I had traveled away from you*. But that wouldn't have been poetic. His image-filled language within the sonnet format creates a beautiful piece of poetry—written for effect as much as for message.

There is wisdom in what C. L. Barber has to say about *The Sonnets* in a 1987 essay, emphasis being on the importance of enjoying them as poetry rather than allowing ourselves to be distracted by intrigue dredged up over time. Barber cites controversy over the identity of persons to whom particular sonnets were written, Shakespeare's relationship to the young man and the dark lady, questions of sexual preference, the identity of the rival poet, and other alluring issues—and then makes this observation about *The Sonnets*:

> Frequently they give compelling utterance to experiences everyone goes through in love—anguish, elation, joy, dismay; and they realize with directness and fullness basic conditions of existence which love has to confront—the fact of mortality, the separateness of human beings, their need

of each other, the graces that come unsought and undeserved. It is better to read the Sonnets for these universal values than to lose their poetry by turning them into riddles about Shakespeare's biography. (1987, 6)

Barber's message: read *The Sonnets* as generic art, not as specific agendas aimed at specific recipients. Reading them as art will allow you to enjoy them and become more insightful about their underlying observations and wisdom.

Shakespeare focused Sonnet 50 intently on one of those "basic conditions of existence" to which Barber refers—the difficulty of separation from a loved one. He captures the feeling of agony and resistance by creating a ponderous tone, beginning in the first quatrain with "how heavy the miles are measured." Beginning with the second quatrain, he uses the horse as the central figure through which to convey that feeling of heaviness and unwillingness. The poor horse "Plods dully on to bear that weight in me," and readers sense that the weight referred to is not just the physical weight on the horse's back, but the rider's emotional weight as well.

Can emotional weight make a horse's task more arduous? Apparently it can—and did. The rider (Shakespeare) imagines that the horse, by some instinct, knows how hesitant he is to put those miles between himself and his friend. Perhaps the rider unconsciously holds the horse back even as he expects the poor beast to press on. Then, instead of feeling grateful for the empathy that he imagines in the horse, he lets his emotion turn to frustration, then to anger—and finally to spurring the poor horse. A hopeless cycle settles into place: the emotion of separation tortures the rider with frustration, the rider tortures the horse with spurs, the horse tortures the rider with groans, and heightened emotion starts the cycle anew.

Is the purpose of this sonnet, as it appears on the surface, to elicit sympathy for its author's stressful experience of coping with separation from his friend? No. Its overriding purpose, as is the case with most of Shakespeare's sonnets, is to say to the sonnet's recipient "I care deeply about you." In this case, the tool Shakespeare uses to deliver that message is a vivid poetic depiction of the sadness he feels upon separation.

Sonnet #66

Tired with all these, for restful death I cry:
As to behold desert a beggar born,
And needy nothing trimmed in jollity,
And purest faith unhappily foresworn,
And gilded honor shamefully misplaced,
And maiden virtue rudely strumpeted,
And right perfection wrongfully disgraced,
And strength by limping sway disabled.
And art made tongue-tied by authority,
And folly (doctor like) controlling skill,
And simple truth miscalled simplicity,
And captive good attending captain ill.
    Tired with all these, from these would I be gone,
    Save that, to die, I leave my love alone.

The Essence of Sonnet #66

My grievances with the human condition are such that
I would gladly lie down and die, just to get away from
it all—except that I would have to leave my love alone.

To fully experience the sonnets visit www.sonnetsofshakespeare.com for a live recording by Darrel Walters.

1st Quatrain

these conditions are too burdensome to live with
[Tired with all these, for restful death I cry:]

chronic poverty
As to behold [desert a beggar born,]

pretense
And [needy nothing trimmed in jollity,]

loss of faith
And [purest faith unhappily foresworn,]

2nd Quatrain

honoring of the dishonorable
And [gilded honor shamefully misplaced,]

sexual abuse
And [maiden virtue rudely strumpeted,]

disrespect for accomplishment
And [right perfection wrongfully disgraced,]

poor stewardship of strength
And [strength by limping sway disabled.]

3rd Quatrain

official stifling of creativity
And [art made tongue-tied by authority,]

disrespect for skill
And [folly (doctor like) controlling skill,]

disrespect for truth
And [simple truth miscalled simplicity,]

unjustifiable servitude
And [captive good attending captain ill.]

Couplet

Tired with all these, from these would I be gone,

selfishly leave you to face all this without me
Save that, to die, I [leave my love alone.]

SONNET 66

Description and Interpretation

As a field of daffodils with a few daisies sprinkled throughout is still known as a field of daffodils, so Shakespeare's collection of sonnets with a few non-sonnets sprinkled throughout is still known as a collection of sonnets. "Sonnet" 66, as it is still called, is one of about a half dozen quasi-sonnets and non-sonnets in the collection of 154. It has fourteen lines and a rhyme scheme that conforms loosely to that of a sonnet, and it is written in the meter of a sonnet: iambic pentameter. Still, it fails to qualify as a pure Elizabethan sonnet for lack of an identifiable series of three quatrains proceeding to a couplet.

Instead, three of this sonnet's lines—the opening line and the closing couplet—have material in common, and eleven independent single lines are sandwiched between. Those eleven lines each cite a human failing that contributes to Shakespeare's disillusionment with the human condition. Together they create a feeling of serial movement through a list rather than a typical sonnet's feeling of single-topic development through three quatrains and a couplet. Sonnet 66, given all its negative portrayals of human activity, amounts to Shakespeare's the-world-is-going-to-hell-in-a-hand-basket statement. Hallett Smith, in *Elizabethan Poetry*, refers to it, along with Sonnets 29 (p. 80) and 30 (p. 24), as one of Shakespeare's "sonnets of despondency." (1952, 182)

Imagine that Shakespeare, at a time when he had his mind programmed to write sonnets, was struck by melancholy thoughts about the frailties of humankind. The somber material overtaking his thinking said *essay*, but his commitment to the form with which he was working at the time said *sonnet*. So he took on the challenge of setting down his grievances with humankind in sonnet form. Even though the sonnet's conventions were incompatible with his content, Shakespeare—poised to say what was on his mind—forged ahead and created this quasi-sonnet. Further, he found a way to shoe-horn into the piece a reference to the classic topic of Elizabethan sonnets: love. *I'll declare*, he thought, *that I would be willing to escape this fouled-up world through death—except for my noble reluctance to leave one whom I love to face this mess without me.*

This fanciful account of Shakespeare's writing of Sonnet 66 might be off the mark, but whatever the story behind this sonnet, love is plainly not at center stage. The author of any good piece of writing works from a spark of inspiration, and Shakespeare's poignant, insightful list of grievances suggests that the spark for this sonnet was his disillusionment with the human condition.

What was it about the society around him that irritated and depressed Shakespeare so profoundly as to prompt the writing of Sonnet 66? He was saddened by the fact of many people being born with nothing and living their lives without ever having a chance for more (desert a beggar born). Bothering him also were persons who—instead of making something worthwhile of themselves—gave empty appearances that they had the world by the tail (needy nothing trimmed in jollity), and he mourned the crushing of noble spirits by a cruel, oppressive world (purest faith unhappily forsworn).

Shakespeare saw underlings bow and scrape to people unworthy of the honor, simply to gain favor with them (gilded honor, shamefully misplaced), and he saw young maidens whose virtue was not honored, but who were instead prostituted (maiden virtue rudely strumpeted). He railed at those who tried to elevate themselves by denigrating people who were in the right (right perfection wrongfully disgraced), and at the weakening of people who showed strength (strength by limping sway disabled). He decried the stifling of creativity by those in power (art made tongue-tied by authority), and the leashing of skill by fools in positions of control (folly, doctor-like, controlling skill). He revered simple truth that was too-often cast aside as overly simple (simple truth, miscalled simplicity), and he ached on behalf of good people forced to serve not-such-good people (captive good attending captain ill).

What marvelous examples Shakespeare gives us here of profound, complex thoughts crafted into concise statements! They are nothing short of masterful. They are also unsettling. Human nature appears to have remained extraordinarily constant across these many centuries. Four hundred years have passed since Shakespeare made these observations, and every condition he cites stares us in the face yet today. Maybe some of the insight we should take from old writings is that we would be wise to act on insights we already have.

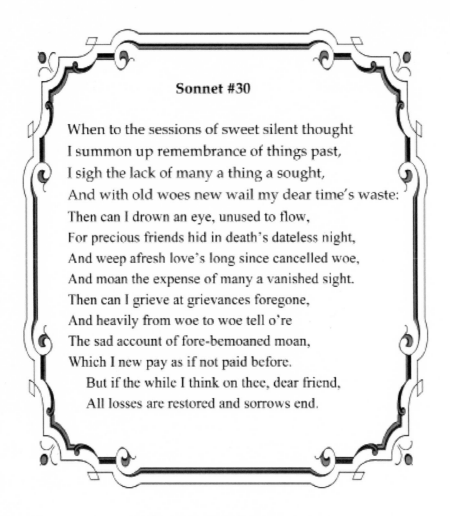

Sonnet #30

When to the sessions of sweet silent thought
I summon up remembrance of things past,
I sigh the lack of many a thing a sought,
And with old woes new wail my dear time's waste:
Then can I drown an eye, unused to flow,
For precious friends hid in death's dateless night,
And weep afresh love's long since cancelled woe,
And moan the expense of many a vanished sight.
Then can I grieve at grievances foregone,
And heavily from woe to woe tell o're
The sad account of fore-bemoaned moan,
Which I new pay as if not paid before.
    But if the while I think on thee, dear friend,
    All losses are restored and sorrows end.

The Essence of Sonnet #30

When I think of losses I have suffered—and at the
same time think of you—I realize that your friendship
compensates for all else, and removes my sorrow.

To fully experience the sonnets visit www.sonnetsofshakespeare.com for a
live recording by Darrel Walters.

Diagram for Greater Understanding

1st Quatrain

When to the sessions of sweet silent thought

call to mind
I [summon up] remembrance of things past,

regret missed opportunities
I [sigh the lack of many a thing a sought,]

cry anew over past failures
And [with old woes new wail my dear time's waste:]

2nd Quatrain

weep　　　**I seldom weep**
Then can I [drown and eye,] [unused to flow,]

deceased loved ones
For [precious friends hid in death's dateless night,]

sadness over a failed love relationship
And weep afresh [love's long since cancelled woe,]

changes to places I held dear
And moan the expense of [many a vanished sight.]

3rd Quatrain

wrongs ignored
Then can I grieve at [grievances foregone,]

mournfully　　　**retell**
And [heavily] from woe to woe [tell o're]

wrongs not ignored
The sad account of [fore-bemoaned moan,]

pay for again by thinking about them
Which I [new pay] as if not paid before.

Couplet

But if the while I think on thee, dear friend,

your friendship compensates for all losses
[All losses are restored and sorrows end.]

SONNET 30

Description and Interpretation

Sonnets 30 and 29 (p. 80) have in common a theme of regret and self-rebuke, but they differ in one fundamental respect. In Sonnet 29, Shakespeare longs to be better, to be more like others whom he respects. In Sonnet 30, he simply recounts unfortunate events throughout his life, many of which were not of his own making. I chose to place Sonnet 29 in the category Declaring Devotion, which he does very strongly in the couplet of that sonnet. I chose to place Sonnet 30 in the category Living Life's Span because regrets over losses along life's way—like growing older (Sonnet 2), suffering unwanted separations (Sonnet 50), and bearing society's ills (Sonnet 66)—are among challenges that most of us encounter.

Shakespeare's flow of delightfully complementary word sounds makes the first quatrain of this sonnet a joy to speak aloud. You may want try it. In the first two lines, the terms "session" and "summon up" imply that the silent thought Shakespeare refers to is a serious, intentional mulling, not just a few fleeting notions that come to mind. The last line of the first quatrain is packed with rich imagery: "old woes" (previous unhappiness), "new wail" (cry again), and "dear time's waste" (foolish waste of a precious commodity along life's way).

Judging by the characterization of his eye as "unused to flow," one might speculate that Shakespeare had suppressed unhappy thoughts for some time. He may have caught himself by surprise when the thoughts he expresses in Sonnet 30 came to him, or he may have consciously used those "sessions of sweet silent thought" to put himself into an emotional state that would make tears flow again and breathe life into emotions that he knew he had kept buried for too long. No one will ever know the catalyst for his thoughts.

In the second quatrain, Shakespeare recounts regrettable events over which he had no control. Friends are "hid in death's dateless night," a phrase both artful and descriptive, emphasizing that he can never hope to see them again. In his next sad recollection, he doesn't tell how the love he lost came to an end, but the event was unquestionably painful ("weep afresh"). "Many a vanished sight" could refer to any familiar place that he had held dear. To return to a place—with all its familiar buildings and businesses and people—after a long absence is to risk being stunned by how unfamiliar the landscape has become. (Imagine him walking those streets today!)

Emotional intensity rises in the third quatrain as Shakespeare searches for ways to react to all the upheaval that his "sessions of sweet silent thought" have brought to the surface. He acknowledges that he kept silent about some former grievances, and says that he might vent his emotions now by grieving them belatedly. Then he contemplates a step-by-step march through woes that he has confronted and grieved previously, a march that he knows he will make with a heavy heart ("heavily") and pay for again in recollection ("new pay").

Assume that a very intentional Shakespeare did believe that this mind-bound journey would free him in some way—perhaps refresh him emotionally—by unchaining him from experiences that had been holding him prisoner. Two very different outcomes are possible from such a journey, and we can only guess which one he experienced. One possibility is that he cast off as past events those fore-bemoaned moans (previous woes) that he suffers again in his mind ("which I new pay"). He may even have smiled at the irony of double jeopardy, and then good-heartedly returned his thoughts to the present to refresh himself and feel appreciation for his friend. The other possibility is that the paying again for past woes was so painful that he shut down his thought exercise, thrust his mind purposefully into a more pleasant venue, and brought to the surface appreciation for his friend. Either way, the assertion that "If the while I think on thee, dear friend, all losses are restored and sorrows end" is a powerful and heart-warming sentiment for the closing of this sonnet. Perhaps Shakespeare's journey of the mind did lead him to that first outcome—to an energizing appreciation for what he had in his friend.

"Sessions of sweet silent thought" are surely less common in our culture of noise and easy access to entertainment and communication. As healthy and powerful as such sessions with ourselves can be, perhaps one of the woes we suffer today is their scarcity.

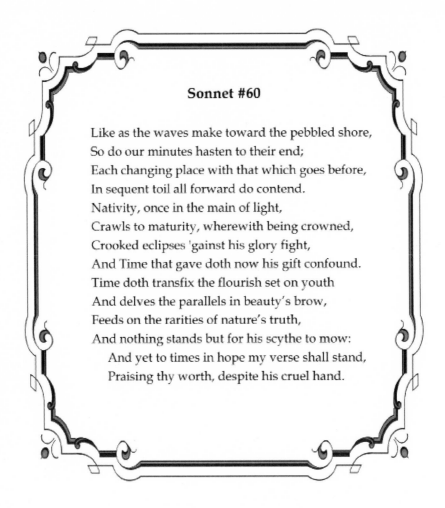

Sonnet #60

Like as the waves make toward the pebbled shore,
So do our minutes hasten to their end;
Each changing place with that which goes before,
In sequent toil all forward do contend.
Nativity, once in the main of light,
Crawls to maturity, wherewith being crowned,
Crooked eclipses 'gainst his glory fight,
And Time that gave doth now his gift confound.
Time doth transfix the flourish set on youth
And delves the parallels in beauty's brow,
Feeds on the rarities of nature's truth,
And nothing stands but for his scythe to mow:
    And yet to times in hope my verse shall stand,
    Praising thy worth, despite his cruel hand.

The Essence of Sonnet #60

Time passes quickly as it befriends the young, persecutes
the old, and ultimately takes away everything. Still, my
praise for you will stand forever.

To fully experience the sonnets visit www.sonnetsofshakespeare.com for a
live recording by Darrel Walters.

Diagram for Greater Understanding

1ˢᵗ Quatrain

Like as the waves make toward the pebbled shore,

So do our minutes hasten to their end;

as one is spent, the next takes its place
[Each changing place with that which goes before,]

minute by minute we press ever forward
[In sequent toil all forward do contend.]

2ⁿᵈ Quatrain

infancy
[Nativity,] once in the main of light,

grows to adulthood   **becoming adult**
[Crawls to maturity,] wherewith [being crowned,]

life's problems   **block progress**
[Crooked eclipses] ['gainst his glory fight,]

impair
And Time that gave doth now his gift [confound.]

3ʳᵈ Quatrain

stop
Time doth [transfix] the flourish set on youth

carves wrinkles into lovely features
And [delves the parallels in beauty's brow,]

ruins nature's beauty
[Feeds on the rarities of nature's truth,]

cuts down everything
And [nothing stands but for his scythe to mow:]

Couplet

but hoping for the best, I forge ahead
[And yet to times in hope my verse shall stand,]

and laud your worth in spite of it all
[Praising thy worth, despite his cruel hand.]

SONNET #60

Description and Interpretation

Shakespeare's strong sense of time passing by, featured prominently in Chapter 6 of this book, is at the core of this sonnet as well.
The overriding difference between this sonnet and the six featured in
chapter 6 is Shakespeare's mindset. In those sonnets, he offers some
countermeasure to time's destructiveness—some recommendation for
fighting back: preserve beauty by describing it in verse or, as we saw in
Sonnet 2 (p. 12), extend your presence by having a child. In this sonnet,
his attitude seems to be *all we can do about Time's punishment is take
what he dishes out and hold on as best we can.* (Note Time's status as
a proper noun, that is, a willful being).

In terms of the classic Elizabethan sonnet form, Sonnet 60 is as
perfect as Sonnet 66 (p. 20) is imperfect. Each of the three quatrains of
this sonnet has a distinct role, and they progress logically from one to
the other. Then the couplet—an entity unto itself—relates back to the
theme that has been developed through the quatrains.

The first quatrain is an elaborate, colorful version of an observation
that we hear voiced in simple terms almost daily: "time flies" or "life
is short." Shakespeare pictures life as a swift rush with an abrupt departure, representing it as he does with waves washing onto the shore
and disappearing. He adds momentum with the phrases "hasten to
their end" and "all forward do contend." Rich, descriptive, expansive
language transforms the cliché "time flies" into a thought-provoking,
ominous reality that foreshadows the remainder of the sonnet.

The second quatrain begins a masterful depiction of the changing
role of Time over the span of a person's life. As infants, Shakespeare
points out, we are in the spotlight. Everyone dotes on us, and all things
are yet possible. Then we "crawl" to maturity, physically as infants
and metaphorically as youngsters encountering obstacles and difficulties along the way. Upon being crowned "mature," we are woefully
naïve about the barriers (crooked eclipses) that lie between us and life's
fulfillment. Since childhood we have envisioned the glory that will
be ours in adulthood—all that we will accomplish; all the dreams we
might fulfill. But Time, the good friend who gave us what we needed
to grow and mature, is about to turn on us.

In the third quatrain, Time the child's nutrient becomes Time the adult's poison. The flourish set on youth, the downright bedazzling growth and development that youth could never have had without Time, is about to be transfixed—stopped in its tracks. Time will now hobble us with age-related impediments. We see the sonnet become increasingly brutal as it progresses, from a simple statement of Time's swift passage in the first quatrain, to turning on youth at the point of adulthood in the second, and finally to brutalizing the aging adult and threatening an all-out slaughter of everything and everyone. Time "delves the parallels in beauty's brow," reminiscent of the ominous prediction he makes to his young friend in Sonnet 2 (p. 12):

> When forty winters shall besiege thy brow
> And dig deep trenches in thy beauty's field,
> Thy youth's proud livery, so gazed on now,
> Will be a tattered weed of small worth held.

The damage continues to escalate. Time "Feeds on the rarities of nature's truth," making clear that damage wrought by Time extends to every living thing in all of nature. That line is reminiscent of one from Sonnet 15 (p. 124): "Everything that grows holds in perfection but a little moment." People, animals, plants, trees—everything succumbs to Time.

And then in the last line of the third quatrain, as if unsure that he has made his point unequivocally, Shakespeare administers the coup de grace. He pictures Time swinging that wicked scythe he has always been rumored to carry, destroying everything in his path: "And nothing stands but for his scythe to mow." The picture of hopelessness is complete.

Unpredictability is one of the well-worn tools in Shakespeare's arsenal. Unlike his treatment of couplets in the sonnets found in chapter 6, in this couplet he does not countervail those doleful observations about Time. Instead, he faces Time head on by saying to the recipient of the sonnet, *Time may well tear everything down with his cruel hand, and I may have no way to counter his powerful deeds, but neither will I be cowed and quieted. Let happen what will happen, but that will not stop me from singing your praises.*

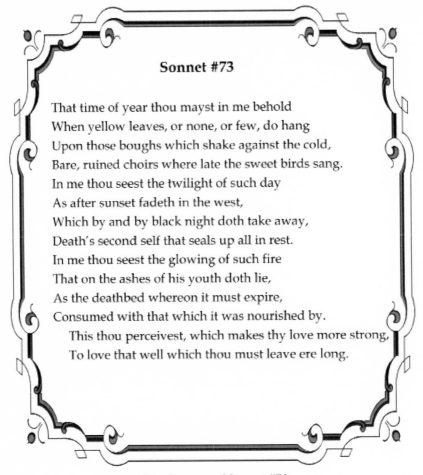

Sonnet #73

That time of year thou mayst in me behold
When yellow leaves, or none, or few, do hang
Upon those boughs which shake against the cold,
Bare, ruined choirs where late the sweet birds sang.
In me thou seest the twilight of such day
As after sunset fadeth in the west,
Which by and by black night doth take away,
Death's second self that seals up all in rest.
In me thou seest the glowing of such fire
That on the ashes of his youth doth lie,
As the deathbed whereon it must expire,
Consumed with that which it was nourished by.
   This thou perceivest, which makes thy love more strong,
   To love that well which thou must leave ere long.

The Essence of Sonnet #73

Because you see that I am near the end of my life,
leaving little time for us to be together, your love
for me is (or should be) stronger than ever.

To fully experience the sonnets visit www.sonnetsofshakespeare.com for a
live recording by Darrel Walters.

Diagram for Greater Understanding

1st Quatrain

you will see if you look at me
That time of year [thou mayst in me behold]

I am in the fall of life
When [yellow leaves, or none, or few, do hang]

limbs losing warmth
Upon those [boughs which shake against the cold,]

limbs past robust times
[Bare, ruined choirs where late the sweet birds sang.]

2nd Quatrain

In me thou seest the twilight of such day

As after sunset fadeth in the west,

turns to total darkness
Which by and by [black night doth take away,]

night signifies the end
[Death's second self that seals up all in rest.]

3rd Quatrain

dying embers
In me thou seest the [glowing] of such fire

what is left of energy-filled fuel
That on [the ashes of his youth] doth lie,

place the last spark will burn out
As the [death-bed whereon it must expire,]

like a fire, life nourishes itself and consumes itself
[Consumed with that which it was nourished by.]

Couplet

seeing this, you will love me more
[This thou perceivest, which makes thy love more strong,]

prizing our time together because so little remains
[To love that well which thou must leave ere long.]

SONNET #73

Description and Interpretation

Shakespeare frequently writes about the transience of all living things. In Sonnet 73, he writes about his own transience, presenting three metaphors that allude to his imminent death. In the end he speculates about the attitude of the sonnet's recipient toward the departure that is now so close in time.

In the first quatrain, Shakespeare presents himself as a tree in late fall, his life span represented by one calendar year. By being noncommittal about the number of yellow leaves left on his boughs, he shows uncertainty about when the end will come. He characterizes his limbs as "boughs which shake against the cold," alluding to death as a transition from warmth to cold, beginning with weakened extremities. Then he summons up thoughts of earlier days, during his prime, when sweet birds sat on his boughs and sang.

His reference to singing birds introduces a specter of the divine, likening the tree (himself) to a cathedral and the boughs to wooden benches where Christian singers sit in rows like birds on boughs. (The box housing singers' benches at the front of a cathedral had been known previously as the "queor," a term later spelled "choir" and applied to the singers themselves.) This bold opening quatrain elicits feelings of empathy, giving witness as it does to the torture of one who faces an unpredictable but imminent demise.

In the second quatrain, the representation of Shakespeare's life span shrinks from a year to a day. He begins, "In me thou seest the twilight," twilight being the period of a day's twenty-four-hour life that corresponds to yellow leaves in the period of a tree's 365-day life. The twilight, "which by and by black night doth take away," represents the harbinger of death, and "black night" becomes "death's second self." We are thereby reminded that twilight, like the time of sparse yellow leaves in the first quatrain, was death's first stage, and death itself the second. He points out graphically that the black night he refers to— death itself—"seals up all in rest."

The glowing of the fire that represents death's imminence in the third quatrain is fundamentally different from and more decisive than the sparsely leaved tree or the day's twilight. A tree can be expected to reawaken the next spring, and daylight can be expected to show itself at the next dawn, but when a fire goes out there is no probability of its being rekindled. A fire is fed by energy-filled wood, and as the act of burning reduces that wood to ash, its residue inexorably consumes the last of itself. Similarly, a life is fed by energy-filled youth, and as the act of living decays that youth, it inexorably consumes the last of itself. Life presupposes death.

Having hammered home, without any doubt, that death awaits, Shakespeare then says to his younger friend *knowing that the time we have left together is not long, surely your love for me will be stronger now*. Because Shakespeare, of the two of them, is the one expected to leave, his ending the sonnet with "which thou must leave ere long" is curious. Some speculate that it should read "which thou must *lose* ere long," but to edit Shakespeare is a tricky and audacious business.

An alternate theory changes the entire meaning of the sonnet. That theory says that Shakespeare is referring not to himself and his demise, but to his youthful vitality and its demise, along with the loss of youthful capabilities. When he admonishes the young man to "love that well which thou must leave ere long," he is saying *love, appreciate, and use well the youthful vigor that you will inevitably lose.*

So what is it that the young man must lose, and therefore love and appreciate all the more—his friend or his youth? The fact that Shakespeare most likely wrote these sonnets in the 1590s, when he was about age thirty, argues for the alternate theory. He could hardly have been feeling the burden of old age and imminent death at that point in his life!

Still, the argument for the first theory is not so easily dismissed. The sonnet that follows this one, Sonnet 74, makes clear that Shakespeare was in fact referring to literal death in Sonnet 73. Apparently he was just taking artistic license to portray his death as imminent when in reality it was not. That allows for the possibility that he did not create this sonnet principally as a personal message to the young man, but perhaps more so as an imaginative piece of generic art.

Sonnet #74

But be contented: when that fell arrest
Without all bail shall carry me away,
My life hath in this line some interest
Which for memorial still with thee shall stay.
When thou reviewest this, thou dost review
The very part was consecrate to thee.
The earth can have but earth, which is his due;
My spirit is thine, the better part of me.
So then thou hast but lost the dregs of life,
The prey of worms, my body being dead,
The coward conquest of a wretches knife,
Too base of thee to be remembered.
    The worth of that is that which it contains,
    And that is this, and this with thee remains.

The Essence of Sonnet #74

When my body leaves you in death, be content to know
that the best part of me stays with you in memorial. That
part—which I consecrate to you—is preserved in my verse.

To fully experience the sonnets visit www.sonnetsofshakespeare.com for a
live recording by Darrel Walters.

Diagram for Greater Understanding

1st Quatrain

ferocious
But be contented: when that [fell] arrest

with no release (death)
[Without all bail] shall carry me away,

I live in this writing
[My life hath in this line some interest]

forever
Which [for memorial] still with thee shall stay.

2nd Quatrain

When thou reviewest this, thou dost review

I've written for you
The very part [was consecrate to thee.]

The earth can have but earth, which is his due;

the part of greatest importance
My spirit is thine, [the better part of me.]

3rd Quatrain

the trivial
So then thou hast but lost [the dregs of life,]

a mere substance
[The prey of worms,] my body being dead,

easily destroyed
[The coward conquest of a wretches knife,]

too common for you to even think about
[Too base of thee to be remembered.]

Couplet

my body was only a vessel for the best of me
[The worth of that is that which it contains,]

you have that best in my writing
And that is this, and [this with thee remains.]

SONNET #74

Description and Interpretation

At a time when Shakespeare was not much older than thirty, he would have had to take considerable poetic license in Sonnet 73 to allude to his own death as imminent. Apparently he did just that, projecting himself into the role of old age. That adds fuel to the argument that some of his sonnet writing may have been as much a matter of creating art as writing for personal reasons.

The opening of Sonnet 74 provides unmistakable evidence that Shakespeare was, in Sonnet 73, referring to the end of his life rather than merely the end of his youth.

> But be contented when that fell arrest
> Without all bail shall carry me away.

One who is locked away in death has no hope of being released, so he likens death to an arrest with no hope of bail. Later, when he uses the words "my body being dead," he leaves absolutely no room for debate about the meaning of Sonnet 73. The alternate theory, that Shakespeare had been writing about the demise of his youth, holds water only if we disregard Sonnet 74.

Sonnets 73 and 74 are for all practical purposes a single poem—a kind of double sonnet that presents an antecedent followed by its consequence. The contrast in tone between the two is striking. Think of the psychological ramifications of facing surgery, with a period of quiet concern leading to the event and a period of stability following. The effect of Sonnets 73 and 74, read as a single poem, is similar. Sonnet 73 presents a solemn buildup to the event (death), and Sonnet 74 presents a vivid depiction of circumstances that should fall into place afterward. In the one, Shakespeare puts a perspective on his relationship with the young friend, and in the other he tries to gain credibility by casting himself as a postmortem spokesman for his own deceased self.

Early in Sonnet 74, Shakespeare begins to make a case for the importance of the poetry that he will leave behind. Positioning himself postmortem, he says that his life remains vital in the lines he has written, and will in fact remain so for memorial. *I've consecrated this to you*, he says, and he urges the young friend to understand that physical life, by comparison, is of little value. "The earth can have but earth," he says, yielding to the ground the body that will unquestionably reside there. Then he says, "My spirit is thine," and adds "the better part of me." The feeling of triumph in that declaration seems to call for an exclamation point. Shakespeare might have used one had its meaning been the same then as today. Introduced into the English language only a century or so earlier, the exclamation point was interpreted then as a note of admiration.

In the third quatrain, Shakespeare devalues the physical body further by reducing its status to that of a mere substance ("the prey of worms"), and he emphasizes that its vulnerability is such that it can be destroyed in a flash ("the coward conquest of a wretches knife"). He observes that these events, worms and coward's knives, are too base (too common) for his young friend to even bring to mind. *The real worth of my body,* he says, *was simply as a container for all that it produced, most specifically what you are reading here—and this remains with you.*

At the time this sonnet was written, its author was relatively unknown, while the young nobleman to whom he is supposed to have addressed it (identity unknown; station in life fairly certain) was prominent. Shakespeare would have been motivated by genuine admiration for the young man, but also, to no small extent, by the realization that a budding artist must cultivate mutual admiration and trust between himself and an influential nobleman if he is to enjoy support for his work. Throughout the sonnets, that relationship accounts for many self-effacing statements coupled with praise for the virtues of the sonnet's recipient.

Political considerations and the language of compliment and fashion notwithstanding, Shakespeare's love and admiration for the young man to whom he addressed many of his sonnets appears time and again to be genuine. In this eloquent and beautiful Sonnet 74, by disparaging the value of his body and elevating the value of his spirit, Shakespeare seems to be saying to whomever reads it, *I want you to read these poems after I'm gone, and continue to love me through them and know that in a spiritual sense I am still with you.*

Pyrame et Thisbe. 26

1985-52-41128

Thesée et Ariadne. 42

Thyself away art present still with me;
For thou not farther than my thoughts canst move,
And I am still with them, and they with thee.

—*from Sonnet 47*

CHAPTER 3

Seeing the Unseen
Sonnets 47, 27, 61, 113, 43, and 24

In these sonnets, Shakespeare calls vivid images to his mind's eye in a variety of circumstances. The images in all six of these sonnets are of his "love," a friend to whom he is devoted. Most scholars believe the person to be a young man, and the relationship to have been a typical sixteenth-century friendship and devotion between young men of noble minds rather than any manner of romantic love. It was also, according to the opinions of most scholars, a relationship between a budding young artist and a still-younger nobleman whose influence as a patron might have been extremely valuable to Shakespeare. Therefore, of all the praise and flattery that flowed from Shakespeare's pen, how much was sincere and how much was political—or for that matter, how much was artistic expression simply for the sake of art—will forever remain unknown.

Sonnets 47, 27, 113, and 43 are accounts of his creating an image in his friend's absence out of a strong desire to see him. Sonnet 61 is a disturbing account of jealousy and soul-searching. Sonnet 24 is a complex quest to know the young man more fully than the mere conjuring of an image.

Each of us sees that which is not actually before the eye from time to time, whether by visualization, imagination, or hallucination. Probably Shakespeare's visualizations were fundamentally similar to what we experience, but the impression given by these sonnets is that they were not—that they were something more. His dramatic descriptions sound almost paranormal at times. That should dissuade us from taking him literally. Probably more than anything he is mixing exaggeration with fabrication to make a point through artistic license that his friend is important to him—that he misses him when they are apart (and covets his support as a patron).

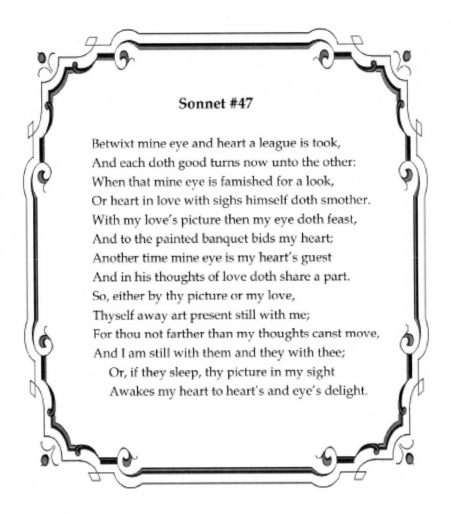

Sonnet #47

Betwixt mine eye and heart a league is took,
And each doth good turns now unto the other:
When that mine eye is famished for a look,
Or heart in love with sighs himself doth smother.
With my love's picture then my eye doth feast,
And to the painted banquet bids my heart;
Another time mine eye is my heart's guest
And in his thoughts of love doth share a part.
So, either by thy picture or my love,
Thyself away art present still with me;
For thou not farther than my thoughts canst move,
And I am still with them and they with thee;
    Or, if they sleep, thy picture in my sight
    Awakes my heart to heart's and eye's delight.

The Essence of Sonnet #47

My eye and heart, separate as they are, have formed a
league between them. They work together to help me
feel your presence when you are away.

To fully experience the sonnets visit www.sonnetsofshakespeare.com for a
live recording by Darrel Walters.

Diagram for Greater Understanding

1st Quatrain

a partnership is formed
Betwixt mine eye and heart [a league is took,]

And each doth good turns now unto the other:

longs to see you
When that mine eye [is famished for a look,]

is sad about separation
Or heart in love [with sighs himself doth smother.]

2nd Quatrain

With my love's picture then my eye doth feast,

that "feast"
And to [the painted banquet] bids my heart;

Another time mine eye is my heart's guest

with the heart's help, visualizes you
And [in his thoughts of love doth share a part.]

3rd Quatrain

So, either by thy picture or my love,

Thyself away art present still with me;

For thou not farther than my thoughts canst move,

And I am still with them and they with thee;

Couplet

if the heart's thoughts are inactive
Or, [if they sleep], thy picture in my sight

Awakes my heart to heart's and eye's delight.

SONNET 47

Description and Interpretation

Shakespeare uses personification in a very sweet way here. He gives individual identities to his eye and his heart. Then, in the sonnet's opening line, he describes their relationship: "Betwixt mine eye and heart a league is took." *My eye and my heart have formed an eye-heart union. They enjoy their own roles, but at the same time each supports the needs of the other.* These two willful entities, the eye and the heart, then proceed to work cooperatively throughout the remainder of the sonnet to make the unseen seen.

That first line shows the kind of confusion caused by changes in grammatical convention over the centuries. Today we would write either "they have formed a league" (active voice) or "a league has been formed" (passive voice). Shakespeare's "a league is took," with its present-tense/past-tense jumble, strikes our eyes and ears as disturbing. All we can do in such places is acknowledge the time warp, adjust to it, and read for meaning rather than grammatical convention. You will find many such bumps in the road as you read the four-hundred-year-old work of Shakespeare—bumps that are well worth the effort they require.

This sonnet is a sequel to Sonnet 46 (not included in this book), in which Shakespeare has the eye and heart quarreling about which should have jurisdiction. Each wants to take control, barring the other. In the couplet, they resolved to share the spoils, assigning ownership of the outer part of an image to the eye and the inner part to the heart. That sets the stage well for the eye and heart to progress from a truce at the end of Sonnet 46 to a spirit of enthusiastic cooperation and mutual benefit at the opening of Sonnet 47.

In the first quatrain, we see reasons for the eye and heart to form a league. When the object of Shakespeare's love is out of sight, the eye becomes "famished for a look." Meanwhile, the heart smothers himself with sighs (sighs in those days being considered a sign of poor health). By casting the eye as famished—needing to be fed—Shakespeare sets himself up to open the second quatrain with two lines of powerful imagery that show eye/heart cooperation:

With my love's picture then my eye doth feast,
And to the painted banquet bids my heart.

How wonderful is that? Shakespeare's eye is "famished" for a look, so the picture of his love becomes a "painted banquet" on which the famished eye feasts. Then the eye, to honor his agreement with the heart, enables the heart to join in the feast, and thus chase away those sighs. In the last two lines of the quatrain, the heart reciprocates by conjuring up feelings of love, thereby enabling the eye to see his absent love through visualization. This second quatrain may be one of the most beautiful and imaginative four-line expressions in all of *The Sonnets*. Surely millions of people across the centuries have said "feast your eyes on this" without knowing they were borrowing from Shakespeare.

In the last three lines of the third quatrain, he expresses a common sentiment, *I'll think about you while you're gone*, but he does so in an impressively elaborate fashion:

Thyself away art present still with me;
For thou not farther than my thoughts canst move,
And I am still with them and they with thee.

The couplet then reminds us that the league cited in the first line is functioning well. The heart is responsible for those thoughts of love expressed so elegantly in the third quatrain, but what if the heart drops the ball? What if the heart, like a lookout on guard duty, falls asleep at his post? In that case, Shakespeare says in the couplet, the heart's faithful partner—the eye—picks up the slack. The eye, with the picture in its sight, awakens that sleeping heart to the delight of both eye and heart.

Little can be gleaned from this writing about the actual relationship between Shakespeare and the sonnet's recipient. Is their relationship strong? Do they see each other frequently? Does the eye become famished and the heart filled with sighs every few days? Or has there been a substantial period of absence at the time of the writing, and is Shakespeare protesting it here with the terms "famished" and "sighs" and "Thyself away?" In short, we don't know whether he is flattering his friend with everyday thoughts or using this verse to impress upon the friend how greatly he is burdened by lengthy separations.

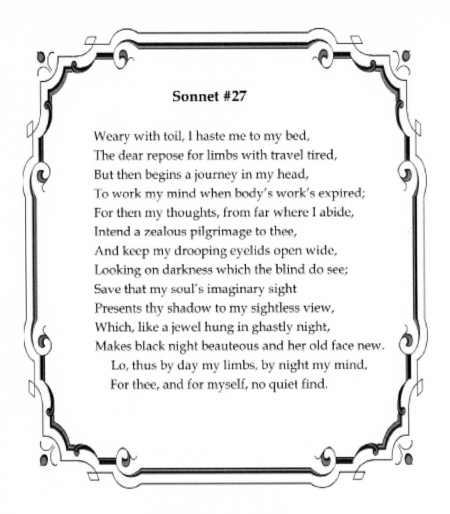

Sonnet #27

Weary with toil, I haste me to my bed,
The dear repose for limbs with travel tired,
But then begins a journey in my head,
To work my mind when body's work's expired;
For then my thoughts, from far where I abide,
Intend a zealous pilgrimage to thee,
And keep my drooping eyelids open wide,
Looking on darkness which the blind do see;
Save that my soul's imaginary sight
Presents thy shadow to my sightless view,
Which, like a jewel hung in ghastly night,
Makes black night beauteous and her old face new.
      Lo, thus by day my limbs, by night my mind,
      For thee, and for myself, no quiet find.

The Essence of Sonnet #27

While traveling far away from you, I have no quiet time.
As soon as I go to bed to rest my body, my mind starts
working to bring your image to me in the dark of night.

To fully experience the sonnets visit www.sonnetsofshakespeare.com for a
live recording by Darrel Walters.

Diagram for Greater Understanding

hurry
Weary with toil, I [haste me] to my bed,

resting place
The dear [repose] for limbs with travel tired,

But then begins a journey in my head,

the day's work is done
To work my mind when [body's work's expired;]

1ˢᵗ Quatrain

am now
For then my thoughts, from far where I [abide,]

an impassioned journey
Intend [a zealous pilgrimage] to thee,

And keep my drooping eyelids open wide,

pure blackness
Looking on [darkness which the blind do see;]

2ⁿᵈ Quatrain

visualization
Save that my soul's [imaginary sight]

your image
Presents [thy shadow] to my sightless view,

Which, like a jewel hung in ghastly night,

removes my darkness
[Makes black night beauteous and her old face new.]

3ʳᵈ Quatrain

Lo, thus by day my limbs, by night my mind,

[For thee,] and for myself, no quiet find.

Couplet

open to interpretation: see end of description, p. 49.

SONNET 27

Description and Interpretation

Traveling across the English countryside at the end of the sixteenth century was difficult and exhausting. In addition to physical wear and tear, travelers had to wrestle with the emotional challenge of being out of sight and out of contact with loved ones. (Where's a good cell phone when you need one?) That angst of separation was the subject of Shakespeare's lament in Sonnet 50 (p. 16): "Thus far the miles are measured from thy friend."

So this sonnet shows that the journey he wrote about in Sonnet 50 was not his first commentary on separation due to travel. His solution to the angst of separation here is to find a way to see his unseen friend despite the distance—to call upon his "imaginary sight" to stand in for what is physically unavailable to him.

Shakespeare opens Sonnet 27 with comments about the weariness that travel imposes on him:

> Weary with toil, I haste me to my bed,
> The dear repose for limbs with travel tired.

There is nothing unusual or unexpected there. Anyone who had spent the day on horseback would look forward to crawling into bed at night. It is the last two lines of the first quatrain that indicate the direction this sonnet is taking:

> But then begins a journey in my head,
> To work my mind when body's work's expired.

As much as the body deserves to be renewed by sleep after a day's work, it will be kept awake by a restless mind.

The implication of the first quatrain—that the journey in Shakespeare's head began involuntarily rather than that he began it—suggests that this nocturnal mental journey was imposed on him. That impression changes in a flash when he says in the second quatrain that his thoughts "intend a zealous pilgrimage to thee." Three terms in that beautifully poetic phrase imply a voluntary mental journey. To "intend" is to have a specific plan in mind. To carry out a "zealous" pilgrimage is to act with enthusiasm and diligence. To make a "pilgrimage" is to travel because of a religious, or at least passionate, devotion. The cumulative impression, then—unless one is willing to divorce Shakespeare's thoughts entirely from Shakespeare's person—is that the journey did not just "begin," as if out of his control, but that he initiated it.

Still, Shakespeare meant full well to say that he considered the experience involuntary. Enter his penchant for creating willful beings of the inanimate, as he often does with Time. In this case, despite writing *thoughts* rather than *Thoughts*, he portrays his thoughts as entirely willful. It was not Shakespeare but Shakespeare's thoughts that *intended* the zealous pilgrimage. (Imagine a murder defense: "It was not I who intended to kill him, judge; it was my thoughts!) His contention is that his thoughts were outside his control, and that they kept his "drooping eyelids open wide" and forced him to look on "darkness which the blind do see." That description of darkness sounds extreme, but prior to ubiquitous street lights, cable boxes, and other electronic gadgets, total darkness of the kind he describes did reign.

In that total darkness, his soul's imaginary sight (also a willful being) presents his friend's "shadow" (visualized image) to his "sightless view." Shakespeare lays all responsibility for these events on his thoughts and on his imaginary sight, while he innocently enjoys what those independent, willful entities have presented to him. He sees in the image of his friend a "jewel" that makes "black night beauteous and her old face new."

So Shakespeare's message to his friend is this: *Worn out as I am all day with my responsibilities, and kept awake as I am all night by images of you, I can't find peace and quiet anywhere*. His words sound on the surface like a complaint, or at least a whine, but one senses an underlying sense of pride. He has let his friend know that he is loyal and committed—that he is in earnest about their friendship.

Curiously, Shakespeare says he has been unsuccessful in finding quiet for both of them: "for thee, and for myself." "For thee" may mean only "on your behalf," in which case Shakespeare would be expecting the problem of insomnia to be his alone. Another possibility, though, is that he senses a two-way communication across the miles. "For thee" may signal a suspicion that he and his friend are having mutual and simultaneous experiences related to their separation, perhaps through a phenomenon that three centuries later would come to be known as telepathy.

Sonnet #61

Is it thy will thy image should keep open
My heavy eyelids to the weary night?
Dost thou desire my slumbers should be broken
While shadows like to thee do mock my sight?
Is it thy spirit that thou sendst from thee
So far from home into my deeds to pry,
To find out shames and idle hours in me,
The scope and tenor of thy jealousy?
Oh no. Thy love, though much, is not so great;
It is my love that keeps mine eye awake,
Mine own true love that doth my rest defeat
To play the watchman ever for thy sake.
    For thee watch I whilst thou dost wake elsewhere,
    From me far off, with others all too near.

The Essence of Sonnet #61

While away, do you send your spirit to my bedside to spy
on me out of jealousy? No. I think I keep myself awake,
worrying about your faithfulness to me.

To fully experience the sonnets visit www.sonnetsofshakespeare.com for a
live recording by Darrel Walters.

Diagram for Greater Understanding

Do you want your image to
[Is it thy will thy image should] keep open

1st Quatrain

My heavy eyelids to the weary night?

want to keep me awake
Dost thou [desire my slumbers should be broken]

make a fool of me
While shadows like to thee do [mock my sight?]

2nd Quatrain

Is it thy spirit that thou sendst from thee

to spy on me
So far from home [into my deeds to pry,]

judge how I spend my time
To [find out shames and idle hours in me,]

extent   nature
The [scope] and [tenor] of thy jealousy?

3rd Quatrain

Oh no. Thy love, though much, is not so great;

It is my love that keeps mine eye awake,

Mine own true love that doth my rest defeat

To play the watchman ever for thy sake.

open to
interpretation: see
description, p. 53.

Couplet

[For thee watch I] whilst thou dost wake elsewhere,

people I don't trust
From me far off, with [others all too near.]

SONNET 61

Description and Interpretation

Sonnet 61 and the sonnet that precedes it here, Sonnet 27, might be considered companions. In both, Shakespeare was kept awake by seeing his dear friend's image. Three differences in Sonnet 61 are important. First, it is the friend who is away and Shakespeare who is at home. Second, Shakespeare perceives the image as disturbing rather than comforting. And third, he sees the image originating from his friend rather than from himself. These conditions support speculation from the end of Sonnet 27's descriptive narrative: Shakespeare may indeed have believed in what we would call today a telepathic phenomenon—or at least he may have wanted to portray himself so.

This sonnet opens with Shakespeare literally asking questions of his far-away friend in response to seeing the image. "Is it thy will?" *Are you purposely trying to keep me from falling asleep?* Again he uses one of his favorite terms to describe a vision—"shadow"—but this time in plural. The impression is that multiple images appear now and then, here and there, as if in some form of haunting. He makes clear that the images are not paying a loving visit, or even a friendly one. His sleep is being disrupted "while shadows like to thee do mock my sight." He finds them invasive.

In the second quatrain, his accusations become more pointed. He refers to the object of his insomnia as "thy spirit," implying that a haunting apparition pursues him from afar. He asks if the spirit is there to pry into his deeds, to "find out shames and idle hours in me." His mental state seems to shift to full-blown paranoia. He accuses the friend of spying on him, as if the "spirit" could see, hear, and report back.

At the end of the second quatrain, Shakespeare conjectures about his young friend's motive. He comments on "the scope and tenor of thy jealousy." *You have your spirit poking into the details of my life while you're on the road, as if you can't trust me to live a life that you approve unless you're here to keep an eye on me.*

The shift in Shakespeare's tone in quatrain three is dramatic. Knowing that he loves with greater zeal than does his friend, he senses that the jealous rage was his—that he had transferred his own feelings of jealousy onto his friend:

> Oh no. Thy love, though much, is not so great;
> It is my love that keeps mine eye awake,
> Mine own true love that doth my rest defeat.

Shakespeare may have been sincerely confronting himself, or he may have been presenting a show for a potential patron. It would be in character with other sonnets if he were simply making an exaggerated attempt to impress his young friend with the extent of his devotion.

The couplet leaves readers with questions. What is he trying to portray with "For thee watch I"? Is this a show of devotion: *I'm so eager to see you that I'm watching for your return*? Or is it a show of jealousy: *I'll be relieved to have you back here, and away from others whose motives I question*? The last line implies jealousy: "From me far off, with others all too near."

And there is yet another possibility. "For thee watch I" might mean something entirely different than watching for his friend's return. He might mean *you don't have to keep an eye on me, because I'm doing that for you. I'm watching myself (monitoring myself) on your behalf.* In modern street language, *I've got it covered.*

Finally, let's talk about the elephant in the room. Why would Shakespeare talk of love and jealousy between himself and his young male friend if he was heterosexual, as scholars generally believe he was on the basis of ample evidence? In Harold Bloom's collection of essays, *Modern Critical Interpretations*, C. L. Barber states in "An Essay on Shakespeare's Sonnets" that "Elizabethans used the term lover between men without embarrassment." He says further of Elizabethan males, "Because their masculinity never was in doubt, men could wear their hair long, dress in silks and ruffles, pose for portraits 'leaning against a tree among roses'" (1987, 17). Casting further light on the times, J. W. Lever, in *The Elizabethan Love Sonnet*, says that "this idea of friendship exercised almost as powerful an appeal to the imagination as the rival concept of romantic love" (1956, 164). We must read the sonnets that Shakespeare wrote to his young friend of nobility with that sixteenth-century context in mind.

Sonnet #113

Since I left you, mine eye is in my mind,
And that which governs me to go about
Doth part his function and is partly blind—
Seems seeing, but effectually is out.
For it no form delivers to the heart
Of bird, of flower, or shape which it doth latch;
Of his quick objects hath the mind no part,
Nor his own vision holds what it doth catch;
For if it see the rudest or gentlest sight,
The most sweet favor, or deformed'st creature,
The mountain or the sea, the day or night,
The crow or dove, it shapes them to your feature.
   Incapable of more, replete with you,
   My most true mind thus maketh mine eye untrue.

The Essence of Sonnet #113

When you and I are apart, I see nothing as it is;
my mind alters the appearance of everything
before my eye by imposing your image onto it.

To fully experience the sonnets visit www.sonnetsofshakespeare.com for a live recording by Darrel Walters.

Diagram for Greater Understanding

1st Quatrain

my thoughts override my vision
Since I left you, [mine eye is in my mind,]

my eye
And [that which governs me to go about]

sees only a fraction of what it looks at
[Doth part his function] and is partly blind —

does not
Seems seeing, but [effectually is out.]

2nd Quatrain

my eye is disconnected from my emotions
For [it no form delivers to the heart]

that the eye takes in
Of bird, of flower, or shape [which it doth latch;]

lively   **none are sent to the mind**
Of his [quick] objects [hath the mind no part,]

and images escape the eye quickly
[Nor his own vision holds what it doth catch;]

3rd Quatrain

least pleasant   **most pleasant**
For if it see the [rudest] or [gentlest] sight,

beautiful   **ugly**
The most [sweet favor,] or [deformed'st creature,]

The mountain or the sea, the day or night,

superimposes your image on them
The crow or dove, it [shapes them to your feature.]

Couplet

overflowing
Incapable of more, [replete] with you,

My most true mind thus maketh mine eye untrue.

SONNET 113

Description and Interpretation

An afterimage, an image that continues to appear in one's vision after exposure to the original image has ceased, is a fascinating physical phenomenon. The most common and most vivid occur after one has looked into a bright light, like a camera flash, but short-term memory can create an afterimage even with a less brilliant stimulus. The vividness and the length of time an image lasts depends on how striking it is and how intensely interested the viewer is in it.

In Sonnet 113, Shakespeare writes about a condition that extends beyond the physiological afterimage, to something that might be considered pathological. He doesn't have a vision coming to him through feelings of love as in Sonnet 27 (p. 46) or jealousy as in Sonnet 61 (p. 50). Rather, he claims to be so obsessed with the image of the sonnet's recipient that his mind superimposes it on everything he looks at. His eye, he says, is "effectually out." It has been blinded by his obsession.

Portraying the heart as the seat of feeling, as he invariably does, Shakespeare says that his eye no longer transports lovely visions such as birds and flowers to his heart as it once did. His mind and heart have a strong connection, but his eye is out of the loop. A blockage (the persistent image of his friend) keeps objects that his eye perceives from being relayed to either the mind or the heart. "Of his [the eye's] quick objects [whatever moves before the eye] hath the mind no part." He says further that the eye itself doesn't even hold onto what it sees for any length of time.

Then Shakespeare launches into a litany of specific visual contrasts that the eye is no longer capable of perceiving. It can no longer distinguish between that which is unpleasant (rude) and that which is pleasant (gentle). Nor can it distinguish between that which is beautiful (sweet favor) or ugly (deformed'st creature). Then he exaggerates beyond believability, as he so often does, to drive his point home: it cannot distinguish between the mountain or the sea, the day or the night, a crow or a dove!

Why is Shakespeare's eye supposedly unable to make all these visual distinctions? According to him, it's because the image of the sonnet's recipient is so vivid and so dear to him that he refuses to let it be replaced with whatever is before his eye at the time. He sees what he wants most to see, and therefore superimposes the image that he is carrying in his mind upon everything he encounters.

To drive the point home even more emphatically, he claims that what he is doing—skewing everything he should be seeing—is not something he chooses to do. Oh no. It is completely involuntary. He characterizes himself as "incapable of more." *I couldn't see those things no matter how much I will it.* The reason he gives is that he is "replete" with his love's image. In other words, that image has filled his very consciousness to the brim, leaving no room for anything else to be let in.

The phrase at the beginning of the sonnet's last line, "My most true mind," may be a defensive move on Shakespeare's part. With it he may be saying, *I know some of the things I've said here sound crazy, but I'm as sane as can be. My mind—my "most true mind"—is as good as ever. It's just that it's playing tricks on my eye.* He seems to be casting the dysfunction of his eye—which is surely an exaggeration—as a quirk, though an admirable one. It testifies to his devotion. He finally calls his eye "untrue," apparently a word creation designed to convey his meaning (false) while also serving the function of making the couplet rhyme.

In the original version of this sonnet, published in 1609, the last line reads "My most true mind thus maketh mine untrue." Scholars assume that Shakespeare simply made a noun out of the adjective "untrue," as in "I have an untrue" rather than "I have an untruth." Because the sonnet has made abundantly clear that the "untrue" is the eye that has been lying to him, the sonnet has been emended in most printings over the centuries since its original publication to read "maketh mine *eye* untrue." Several such emendations account for small variations in *The Sonnets* from one publication to another. Being aware of that may fend off some confusion as you read *The Sonnets* from various sources.

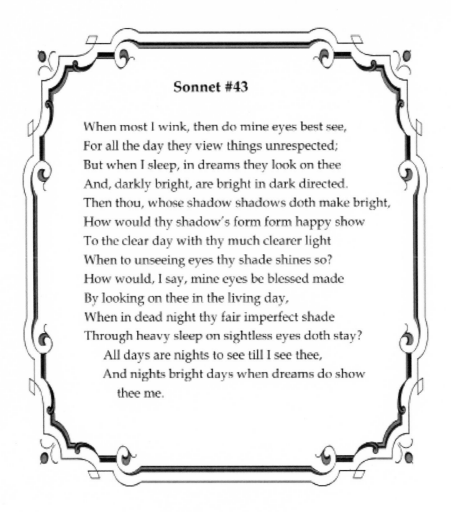

Sonnet #43

When most I wink, then do mine eyes best see,
For all the day they view things unrespected;
But when I sleep, in dreams they look on thee
And, darkly bright, are bright in dark directed.
Then thou, whose shadow shadows doth make bright,
How would thy shadow's form form happy show
To the clear day with thy much clearer light
When to unseeing eyes thy shade shines so?
How would, I say, mine eyes be blessed made
By looking on thee in the living day,
When in dead night thy fair imperfect shade
Through heavy sleep on sightless eyes doth stay?
    All days are nights to see till I see thee,
    And nights bright days when dreams do show
       thee me.

The Essence of Sonnet #43

I see best while asleep, because you are there in my
dreams. How brightly, then, will your image shine when
I see you in living day! Until then, I covet the night.

To fully experience the sonnets visit www.sonnetsofshakespeare.com for a
live recording by Darrel Walters.

Diagram for Greater Understanding

1st Quatrain

with eyelids closed
[When most I wink,] then do mine eyes best see,

outside my interest
For all the day they view things [unrespected;]

But when I sleep, in dreams they look on thee

looking at dark lids   see well
And, [darkly bright,] [are bright] in dark directed.

2nd Quatrain

whose image stands out from the darkness
Then thou, [whose shadow shadows doth make bright,]

look still more impressive
How would thy shadow's form [form happy show]

brighter than daylight
To the clear day with thy much [clearer] light

you are so highly visible
When to unseeing eyes [thy shade shines so?]

3rd Quatrain

how joyous it would be
[How would, I say, mine eyes be blessed made]

to see you in person
[By looking on thee in the living day,]

beautiful but unreal image
When in dead night thy [fair imperfect shade]

Through heavy sleep on sightless eyes doth stay?

Couplet

All days are nights to see till I see thee,

And nights bright days when dreams do show

thee me.

SONNET 43

Description and Interpretation

Shakespeare's separation from his friend is the subject of several sonnets. In Sonnet 50 (p. 16), when a journey puts miles between himself and his friend, he laments "My grief lies onward and my joy behind." In Sonnet 47 (p. 42), he responds to the unavoidable absence of his friend with a mind game: "Thyself away art present still with me, for thou not farther than my thoughts canst move." And in Sonnet 113 (p. 54), he superimposes his friend's image on everything he looks at when his friend is not with him.

In this sonnet, Shakespeare finds yet another way to see the unseen in his friend's absence: he adopts an alternate reality. In a first line that defies what we know to be true, he claims to see best with his eyes closed:

When most I wink, then do mine eyes best see.

That assertion seems nonsensical on the surface, but he explains himself in the remainder of the first quatrain. Everything he looks at during the day, in the absence of his friend, is something that no longer holds any interest for him. Therefore he pays no attention to (shows no respect for) anything around him. He sees what he wants most to see as he sleeps: his absent friend, who appears in his dreams.

As confident and buoyant as Shakespeare sounds initially about the joy he finds in his night visions, his tone later becomes more subdued. He gradually reveals that he knows he is settling for what he can get—that his most earnest desire is to see his friend again in person.

He begins to back down from his cheerful exaltation of dream life by describing his eyes as "darkly bright." They are "bright in dark directed" due to his dreams, but still in the dark, looking at a visualized image—not in the light of day, looking at the real thing

In the second quatrain, he leans on one of his favorite descriptive terms: shadow. In Sonnet 27 (p. 46), the "shadow" was a lovely image of his friend, conjured up while he was trying to fall asleep. In Sonnet 61 (p. 50), the "shadow" was an intrusive image of his friend imposed by jealousy. In this sonnet, "shadow" has the double meaning of *your image* and *the darkness from which your image emerges*: "thou whose shadow shadows doth make bright." Then he makes clear that as much as he enjoys his dreams, his true desire is to see his friend again in the light of day: *If I can see you this vividly with my eyes closed, I can only imagine what a "happy show" that clear light of yours would make in the clear day.*

In two places in the second quatrain, Shakespeare writes consecutive iterations of the same word: "shadow shadows" and "form form." He seems to enjoy this kind of word play. For another example see "music music" in the first line of Sonnet 128 (p. 94).

In the third quatrain, he re-words the second quatrain in an "as I said" statement: "How would, I say, mine eyes be blessed made." He admits further that the dream approach to seeing his friend is insufficient. He describes the dream image as "thy fair imperfect shade." It is "fair" (beautiful) because of whose image it is, and "imperfect" because of its being a visualization rather than the actual person. The eyes that he described earlier as "darkly bright" he now describes as "sightless." *I enjoy seeing you in my dreams, but I know it's only a poor substitute for the real thing. I hope to see you again in the flesh soon.*

Shakespeare doesn't know how much time will pass before he will again see his friend in the "living day." He ends the sonnet with a couplet in the highly exaggerated language that artists in those times typically directed at nobility. "All days are nights to see till I see thee." *In your absence I will treat the day as others treat the night—as a time during which the hours pass unused.* "And nights bright days." *And I will treat the night as others treat the day—as the time in which vital living takes place:* "when dreams do show thee [to] me." (The inexplicable missing *to* is bothersome.) He revels in knowing that each night will treat his "sightless eyes" to a clear image of his friend—an image that outshines all daytime images. He knows also that something better awaits him in the daylight.

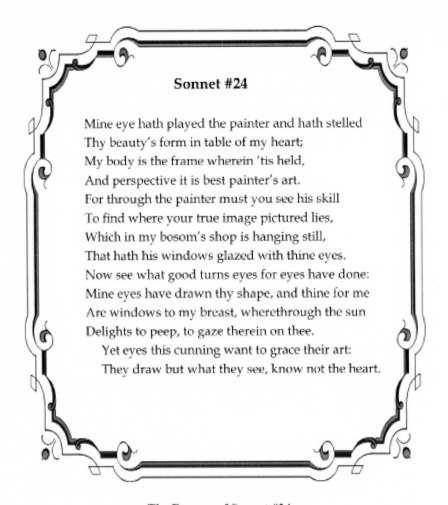

Sonnet #24

Mine eye hath played the painter and hath stelled
Thy beauty's form in table of my heart;
My body is the frame wherein 'tis held,
And perspective it is best painter's art.
For through the painter must you see his skill
To find where your true image pictured lies,
Which in my bosom's shop is hanging still,
That hath his windows glazed with thine eyes.
Now see what good turns eyes for eyes have done:
Mine eyes have drawn thy shape, and thine for me
Are windows to my breast, wherethrough the sun
Delights to peep, to gaze therein on thee.
   Yet eyes this cunning want to grace their art:
   They draw but what they see, know not the heart.

The Essence of Sonnet #24

I have painted a perfect image of you in my heart. Fix
your eyes on it to see your true likeness, and to give to me
(and others) windows through which to see your inner self.

To fully experience the sonnets visit www.sonnetsofshakespeare.com for a
live recording by Darrel Walters.

Diagram for Greater Understanding

engraved

1st Quatrain
Mine eye hath played the painter and hath [stelled]

on my heart's surface
Thy beauty's form [in table of my heart;]

My body is the frame wherein 'tis held,

my perspective on your image is without flaws
And [perspective it is best painter's art.]

2nd Quatrain
For through the painter must you see his skill

To find where your true image pictured lies,

breast
Which in my [bosom's shop] is hanging still,

your eyes as windows
That hath [his windows glazed with thine eyes.]

3rd Quatrain
Now see what good turns eyes for eyes have done:

Mine eyes have drawn thy shape, and thine for me

a way to see you through your eyes
Are [windows to my breast,] wherethrough the sun

shed light on you
Delights to peep, to [gaze therein on thee.]

Couplet

as clever as mine   **capture more than an image**
Yet eyes [this cunning] want to [grace their art:]

do not know you deeply
They draw but what they see, [know not the heart.]

SONNET 24

Description and Interpretation

More than any other sonnet in this book, this one is baffling. Perhaps you can glean more from it than you find written here. Why is it included in this book? Its simultaneous traits of angelic beauty and devilish difficulty are too intriguing to pass up.

Shakespeare begins with a tribute to the beauty of his friend, the sonnet's recipient. Florid language abounds. He could have chosen to say something akin to, *I carry within myself an indelible image of you*, but instead he makes a willful being of his eye. He has done that in other places, as you know from having read Sonnet 47 (p. 42), but here he goes a step further. Using metaphor, he casts his eye as a third party—a painter:

Mine eye hath played the painter and hath stelled
Thy beauty's form in table of my heart.

To emphasize that the image is a part of him, he depicts his body as its frame.

In the last line of the first quatrain, he claims that the perspective in the image he has created is "best painter's art." By the end of the sonnet, however, the incompleteness of the image will be revealed.

The first two lines of the second quatrain sound like a boastful elaboration on the last line of the first quatrain: "For through the painter must you see his skill to find where your true image pictured lies." *I have produced a flawless image of you, one so true that even you—as a result of my skill—could learn something about yourself from it.*

After having already assigned his body the role of frame for the painting, he now characterizes his bosom (the heart's home) as his shop, and the place where the painting hangs. In saying that it was painted there, and hangs there still, he emphasizes that *your image is an indelible part of me.*

The greatest difficulty in interpreting the meaning of this sonnet begins with the last line of the second quatrain. Shakespeare claims that the windows of his shop (bosom) are "glazed with thine eyes." The intrigue builds even more with the opening of the third quatrain: "Now see what good turns eyes for eyes have done." Apparently his eyes and his friend's eyes will in some way serve each other. He elaborates by saying that his eyes have "drawn thy shape," and that the eyes of his friend will serve as "windows to my breast, wherethrough the sun delights to peep, to gaze therein on thee."

The significance of the word "image" now becomes clear. What he has seen and drawn is only the visual representation of his friend, not a comprehensive reality. By way of contrast, the sun—with the help of his friend's eyes—will gaze not simply "on thy image," but "on thee." The implication is that the friend's eyes, illuminated by the sun and then working together with the product of Shakespeare's eyes, will reveal a comprehensive picture of what he had known heretofore as little more than an image.

In the couplet, we see Shakespeare admitting that the perfect image he initially created and crowed about falls short of revealing the full reality of his friend. He says, in effect, *if I am bright enough to perceive your image so perfectly, I am bright enough to want more*:

> Yet eyes this cunning want to grace their art:
> They draw but what they see, know not the heart.

In simplest terms, this sonnet is an elaborate paraphrase of the age-old adage "Beauty is only skin deep."

Questions abound. Is Shakespeare saying that his only chance of seeing his friend fully is to look through the friend's eyes? What is the significance of the sun? One thought is that the sun will open the full view of the friend to the world at large, but that seems unlikely for something as personal as a sonnet. More likely the sun is simply a representation of enlightenment. A reasonable paraphrase of Shakespeare's meaning might be this: *The image I have made, vivid and precise as it is, by itself reveals only the beauty of your physical form. I want to add to my artwork the richest possible understanding of all that you are. With your eyes as the windows to my breast (to my rendering of your image), the sun—shining through your knowledge of yourself—can enhance that image so that it becomes a view of you in all your fullness. That is the complete view that I want for both of us.*

Love alters not with his brief hours and weeks,
But bears it out even to the edge of doom.

—*from Sonnet 116*

Source: Philadelphia Museum of Art
Access Number: 1985–52–30130
Title: The Chat
Source: Dutch, Cornelis de Visscher
Date : 1628–1658

CHAPTER 4

Declaring Devotion
Sonnets 76, 91, 143, 29, 37, and 116

Shakespeare, the all-time master of declaring devotion, does so in many sonnets beyond those shown here. Within this sampling you'll see an impressive array of approaches.

In Sonnets 29 and 91, he compares himself to others in several ways, including the extent of his devotion. In Sonnet 29, sometimes called one of his despondency sonnets, he releases a deluge of self-pity. After telling of the many ways in which he wishes he were like others, he ends with a powerful statement of devotion in which he says he would trade places with no one if it meant having to give up his relationship with the sonnet's recipient. His approach in Sonnet 91, apparently after some maturation on his part, is nearly the opposite. He sounds satisfied with himself. He recounts an array of commonly valued traits and possessions, many of which he coveted in Sonnet 29, and he rejects them as unimportant. His love, he says, is better than all else.

In Sonnets 76 and 37, he makes no comparisons with others. Apparently having been criticized (perhaps by the young man to whom he wrote) for displaying a rather narrow view, in Sonnet 76 he defends the repetitious content of his writing. He says to the sonnet's recipient *you are all I care to write about*. In Sonnet 37, he virtually surrenders his own identity. So devoted is he to the sonnet's recipient that he declares an intent to live vicariously through him—the one on whom he heaps the devotion.

Sonnets 143 and 116 are unique. Sonnet 143 is a one-of-a-kind appeal for attention from the one to whom he is devoted. It is highly unusual and entertaining. Sonnet 116, powerful and timeless, is one of the most quoted and revered of Shakespeare's sonnets. It amounts to a revealing and moving definition of love.

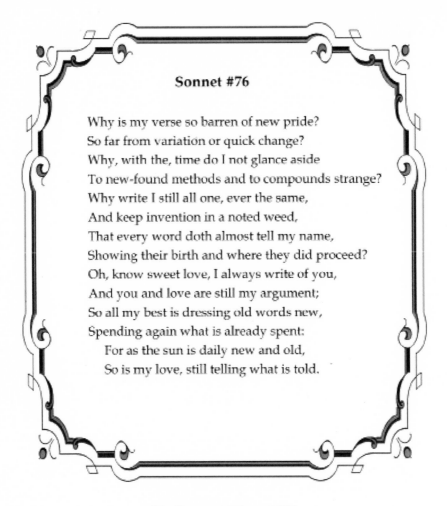

Sonnet #76

Why is my verse so barren of new pride?
So far from variation or quick change?
Why, with the, time do I not glance aside
To new-found methods and to compounds strange?
Why write I still all one, ever the same,
And keep invention in a noted weed,
That every word doth almost tell my name,
Showing their birth and where they did proceed?
Oh, know sweet love, I always write of you,
And you and love are still my argument;
So all my best is dressing old words new,
Spending again what is already spent:
   For as the sun is daily new and old,
   So is my love, still telling what is told.

The Essence of Sonnet #76

Why does my writing lack variation? I am consumed
by thoughts of you and my love for you, and therefore
I write about nothing else.

To fully experience the sonnets visit www.sonnetsofshakespeare.com for a
live recording by Darrel Walters.

Diagram for Greater Understanding

1st Quatrain

lacking in innovation
Why is my verse so [barren of new pride?]

lively
So far from variation or [quick] change?

today's fashion
Why, with [the time,] do I not glance aside

recent trends   novel ideas
To [new-found methods] and to [compounds strange?]

2nd Quatrain

Why write I still all one, ever the same,

predictable box
And keep invention in a [noted weed,]

my very words identity me as the author
That [every word doth almost tell my name,]

my line of thought
Showing [their birth and where they did proceed?]

3rd Quatrain

Oh, know sweet love, I always write of you,

topic
And you and love are still my [argument;]

inventing variations
So all my best is [dressing old words new,]

Spending again what is already spent:

Couplet

cyclical
For as the sun is [daily new and old,]

ever repeating itself
So is my love, [still telling what is told.]

SONNET 76

Description and Interpretation

One interpretation of this sonnet is that Shakespeare is defending himself against charges that he's not keeping up with the times. He feels the heat of successful rival poets and fears the danger of becoming boring and monotonous by comparison. Far from feeling confident, he sees evidence that he's being beaten at this game of poetry. He needs to convince his critics—the young man to whom he has been writing being the principal figure—that he is not rigidly resisting novelty ("barren of new pride"). While others say his work lacks versatility, he defends it as a justifiable display of constant affection.

Another interpretation, perhaps closer to the mark, is that he's thoroughly confident in his work. He's being sarcastic and a bit pugnacious—to the extent that he dares to be within his culturally subservient position. Imagine that others (particularly the young man to whom he writes) have gently commented on the sameness of his writing, and that he is—through a poetic response—answering with exaggerated paraphrases of their comments. Imagine Shakespeare inflating the comments of others in these ways:

Table 4.1.

Criticism Leveled	Shakespeare's Exaggeration
Not as current as you might be	Barren of new pride
Needing some variety	Far from variation or quick change
Not inventive enough	Keep invention in a noted weed
Authorship is recognizable	Every word doth almost tell my name

In his exaggerated account of the criticisms he's heard, Shakespeare seems to be positioning himself throughout the first two quatrains to meet the challenge. *Are these the qualities of my writing that you question? Apparently you don't understand the frame of mind from which I write. I'm going to have to set you straight.* One can imagine him with a raised eyebrow and a suppressed sneer as he writes, all the while trying to remain restrained and respectful despite feeling hurt.

After two quatrains of feeding back in exaggerated form the criticisms that he considers unwarranted, Shakespeare devotes the remainder of the sonnet to justifying—even extolling—what he has been creating. He challenges the young man to understand him. "I always write of you," he says. He seems to be asking his young friend, *don't you recognize that what you're reading is a monument to you?*

Then as he launches into an explanation, a tone of patience and earnestness takes over. He's trying to put some good sense into the head of the young friend who has been blinded by immaturity and impetuousness. *I have no desire to lessen the attention I lavish on you simply to demonstrate that I can put a variety of material into these sonnets. What you are reading is evidence of my sincere devotion. I'll find my variety in style* (dress old words new) *rather than in content, and I'll continue to sing your praises.*

By characterizing words as something to be spent, as if they were a form of currency, he may be embedding into his explanation a subtle analogy. *Money isn't a "compound strange," nor is it anything "new-found." Like the words in my verse, money is familiar to everyone and used repeatedly. Still, you never hear of it being criticized as repetitious or monotonous or overly common. Money is valued for the power it has to purchase goods and services. So too, the words I'm using in my sonnets, familiar to everyone and used repeatedly, have the power to purchase expressions and ideas. It's just that my choice,* says Shakespeare to the less-than-appreciative young man, *is to focus those expressions and ideas on all that I appreciate about you.*

In the couplet, the comparison he makes between the sun and his love for the young man is particularly powerful. The sun is both new and old every day. As we see it come and go—rising in the morning and setting in the evening—we never wish for something different. We appreciate the blessing it delivers each day. *My love for you is like that sun,* he says. *The sun never tries to put on a fashionably different appearance, or rise in the West rather than the East. It never seeks ostentatious adornments beyond the natural beauty that it carries with it at all times. It simply shows itself anew each day. As you appreciate the warmth and comfort that the sun brings to you so faithfully, and never think of its repetition as monotonous or unimaginative, so may you appreciate the warmth and comfort of my recurring praise and my appreciation of you as expressed in these sonnets.*

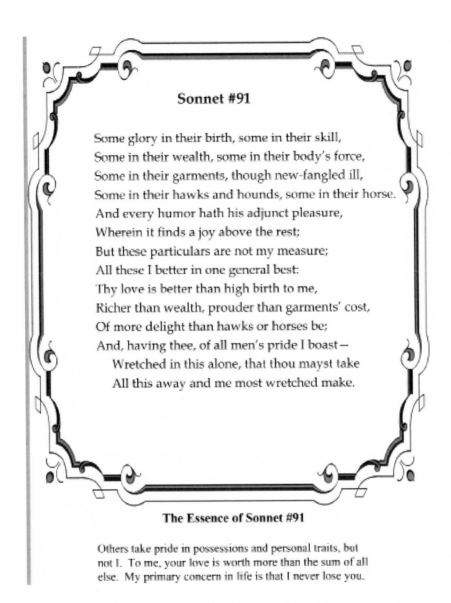

Sonnet #91

Some glory in their birth, some in their skill,
Some in their wealth, some in their body's force,
Some in their garments, though new-fangled ill,
Some in their hawks and hounds, some in their horse.
And every humor hath his adjunct pleasure,
Wherein it finds a joy above the rest;
But these particulars are not my measure;
All these I better in one general best:
Thy love is better than high birth to me,
Richer than wealth, prouder than garments' cost,
Of more delight than hawks or horses be;
And, having thee, of all men's pride I boast—
    Wretched in this alone, that thou mayst take
    All this away and me most wretched make.

The Essence of Sonnet #91

Others take pride in possessions and personal traits, but
not I. To me, your love is worth more than the sum of all
else. My primary concern in life is that I never lose you.

To fully experience the sonnets visit www.sonnetsofshakespeare.com for a
live recording by Darrel Walters.

Diagram for Greater Understanding

ancestry

Some glory in their [birth,] some in their skill,

physical strength

Some in their wealth, some in their [body's force,]

clothing   **just to be fashionable**

Some in their [garments,] though [new-fangled ill,]

trained animals

Some in their [hawks and hounds,] some in their horse.

1ˢᵗ Quatrain

temperament   **added**

And every [humor] hath his [adjunct] pleasure,

Wherein it finds a joy above the rest;

gauge of worth

But these particulars are not my [measure;]

All these I better in one general best:

2ⁿᵈ Quatrain

Thy love is better than high birth to me,

Richer than wealth, prouder than garments' cost,

Of more delight than hawks or horses be;

I am envied

And, having thee, [of all men's pride I boast—]

3ʳᵈ Quatrain

my one worry

[Wretched in this alone,] that thou mayst [take

end our relationship   **miserable**

All this away] and me most [wretched] make.

Couplet

SONNET 91

Description and Interpretation

This is one of the most straightforward and easily understood of *The Sonnets*. The first quatrain is devoted to an account of many factors in life that people find fulfilling. Some put great stock in their lineage: simply having been born into a family of prominence means much to them. Others take pride in what they are able to do—the skills they have acquired. Some are blessed with both high birth and skill, but skill has always been a valued counterweight for those whose family tree is unimpressive. Some like to flaunt wealth, whether inherited or earned, and others take great pride in their physical prowess. Shakespeare has no negative commentary to make about any of those joys, but he does get a bit snarly about people who put great stock in what they wear. The appeal of new apparel, he implies, can be a matter of wanting to be fashionable (new-fangled ill) more so than suitable. Enjoyment in owning and training animals—hawks, dogs, horses—rounds out his account of pleasures that people engage in and enjoy.

He opens the second quatrain with an observation about the great diversity of interests among "men" (used as a generic term). He notes that all of us, with our great variety of temperaments and inclinations (humours), are pursuing something that fills life with meaning. A given person's pleasures and inclinations might run to any one of a number of pursuits, including many outside those that he cites in the first quatrain. Those pleasures, as add-ons (adjunct) to the necessities of life, are sources of great joy for each of us.

Up to this mid-point of the second quatrain, Shakespeare has sounded generally positive and accepting, but the last two lines of the second quatrain ring with a tone of superiority:

> But these particulars are not my measure;
> All these I better in one general best.

At first he seems haughty in saying "All these I better," but once he begins the third quatrain, his "best" sounds laudable and his message more noble:

> Thy love is better than high birth to me,
> Richer than wealth, prouder than garments' cost,
> Of more delight than hawks or horses be.

A happy feeling is infused into the sonnet, and all the particulars of the first quatrain are brought back in the third to emphasize their unfavorable comparison to Shakespeare's love for his friend. He seems to be in a contented, elevated state of mind. With his sense of well-being rising higher and higher, he reaches euphoria.

Then the last line of the third quatrain disappoints. It paints Shakespeare as boastful and condescending. "And having thee, of all men's pride I boast." *The pride I feel in our relationship is superior to the pride that others feel in their relatively petty pleasures. Seeing what I have in you, surely they envy me.* Knowing Shakespeare's penchant for hyperbole in his sonnets may prompt us to dismiss the negative impression he gives. Authors commonly exaggerate out of a strong desire to impress the person to whom they are writing, and Shakespeare was a master of that.

The couplet, however, shows him to have put himself on thin ice. He realizes that his scorn for the inferiority of others' joys relative to his may be misplaced. He has not calculated the possibility of loss, or the misery it might bring. Many of the particulars whose importance he has minimized are more secure than the "one general best" that he displays so prominently. Bloodline, for example, is constant through thick and thin. By contrast, his joy is fragile. What keeps him awake at night? What causes him pangs of anxiety? The thought that everything he values so highly in his precious relationship to his friend could disappear overnight.

> Wretched in this alone, that thou mayst take
> All this away and me most wretched make.

He uses "wretched" in the sense of gloomy, forlorn, and miserable. After having projected himself to the heights, he is seized by awareness that a trip from the heights to the depths is possible—and would be overwhelming.

Such a plunge would be wretched indeed. The higher one rises, the greater the fall if something goes awry. He acknowledges the presence of that danger and probably exaggerates his anticipated wretchedness to impress upon his friend how deeply he values their relationship. He might also have calculated that by emphasizing the importance of their bond he would discourage his young friend and potential patron from weakening it.

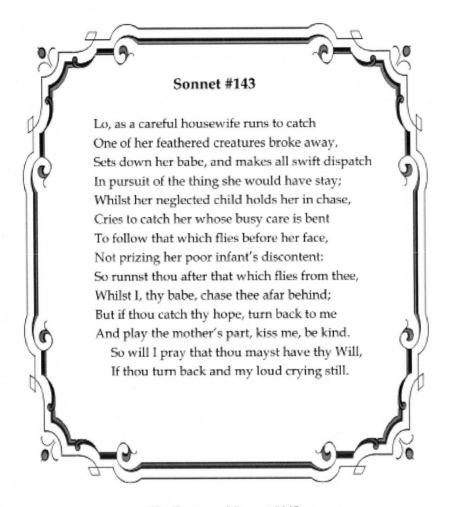

Sonnet #143

Lo, as a careful housewife runs to catch
One of her feathered creatures broke away,
Sets down her babe, and makes all swift dispatch
In pursuit of the thing she would have stay;
Whilst her neglected child holds her in chase,
Cries to catch her whose busy care is bent
To follow that which flies before her face,
Not prizing her poor infant's discontent:
So runnst thou after that which flies from thee,
Whilst I, thy babe, chase thee afar behind;
But if thou catch thy hope, turn back to me
And play the mother's part, kiss me, be kind.
　　So will I pray that thou mayst have thy Will,
　　If thou turn back and my loud crying still.

The Essence of Sonnet #143

I lag behind as you pursue lofty hopes and dreams; but I support you, trusting that you will—in the midst of your successes—keep me in your life and treat me tenderly.

To fully experience the sonnets visit www.sonnetsofshakespeare.com for a live recording by Darrel Walters.

Diagram for Greater Understanding

1ˢᵗ Quatrain

conscientious
Lo, as a [careful] housewife runs to catch

(we'll call it a chicken)   loose from the pen
[One of her feathered creatures] [broke away,]

hurries
Sets down her babe, and [makes all swift dispatch]

the chicken
In pursuit of [the thing she would have stay;]

2ⁿᵈ Quatrain

runs after her
Whilst her neglected child [holds her in chase,]

disposed
Cries to catch her whose busy care is [bent]

the chicken
To follow [that which flies before her face,]

ignoring
[Not prizing] her poor infant's discontent:

3ʳᵈ Quatrain

So runnst thou after that which flies from thee,

Whilst I, thy babe, chase thee afar behind;

get what you're after
But if thou [catch thy hope,] turn back to me

And play the mother's part, kiss me, be kind.

witty double meaning

Couplet

what you're chasing / me
So will I pray that thou mayst have [thy Will,]

calm my distress
If thou turn back and [my loud crying still.]

SONNET 143

Description and Interpretation

Shakespeare scholars generally agree that the late sonnets, beginning with 127, were written to a person whom they dub "the dark lady." Opinions vary as to how much darkness refers to her appearance and how much to her character. She is thought to have beguiled Shakespeare, and she may have been his mistress. His feelings toward her, as shown in the sonnets included in this book, range from early infatuation (Sonnet 128, 94) to disgust over his inability to free his mind of her after she has become a scourge (Sonnet 147, 118).

Sonnet 143 is an oddity in that more than half of it is devoted to a comedic domestic scene that belies the sonnet's true nature. Those first two quatrains give no hint that a serious human relationship lies at its core.

At the outset, a frazzled housewife is trying to meet her responsibilities. She's holding her young child when one of the chickens (interpretation of "feathered creature") in her charge gets loose. She needs to catch it, so she sets the child down. Predictably, the child chases the mother and cries while the mother neglects the child to chase the chicken. All this domestic action is not as detached from Shakespeare's point as it seems. In fact, it sets the very foundation for what he has to say to the lady whose attention he is pursuing.

Beginning in the third quatrain, Shakespeare reveals this frantic housewife scenario as the bedrock of the sonnet. He creates an analogy that shows the purpose—and the brilliance—of those first eight lines. As the child is feeling neglected while chasing its mother, so is he feeling neglected while chasing the woman to whom he is writing:

So runnst thou after that which flies from thee,
Whilst I, thy babe, chase thee afar behind.

This analogy is powerful on the heels of the scenario about the frazzled housewife and distraught child. Several questions come to mind. We know the mother is chasing a chicken, but what is the sonnet's recipient chasing? It could be status or material advantages, or perhaps another man. Why does Shakespeare cast himself as a babe? It may be that he feels helpless, or that he is considerably younger than the woman he is pursuing (Shakespeare scholars have calculated that he was). Or it could be just a matter of his making the analogy work. Why does he consider himself far behind? Is he referring to his lower station, she being a part of the nobility? Or does he know of a specific rival whom he believes to be far ahead in the race for her affection? Questions far outnumber answers, and after four hundred years, the trail is more than a little cold.

Finally, in the middle of the third quatrain, Shakespeare makes his bid. *If you catch whatever it is that you're chasing, so that it no longer occupies your attention, I hope you'll turn back to me.* Then he ties their relationship to the relationship between mother and child. He asks her to "play the mother's part, kiss me, be kind": *Please treat me in the way that the neglectful mother would have treated her child once she was free to attend to it.* There is a pathos in that plea that could bring tears of sympathy to the eyes of a sensitive reader. He seems extraordinarily vulnerable and childlike. How difficult it is to picture this pillar of English literature, Time Magazine's Person of the Millennium, as a lonely, rejected young man starved for kindness and affection!

Some see more in his analogy than simply equating the relationship between a child and mother to the relationship between a man and woman. Shakespeare's picturing the dark lady of his desire as the mother figure and himself as the child opens speculation about the Oedipus complex theorized by Sigmund Freud—the psychological mindset of a child who desires an intimate relationship with the parent of the opposite sex. Considering the mountain of conjecture that has been built on the life and nature of William Shakespeare, one should not be surprised that the Oedipus complex, in a few minds, swirls somewhere among the clouds surrounding that mountain.

In the couplet, Shakespeare shows that he is ready to call upon his wit no matter how serious the topic: "Thou mayst have thy Will." With an uppercase W, he tells the lady, *once you have freed yourself from whatever else you are chasing, you may have me: Will Shakespeare.*

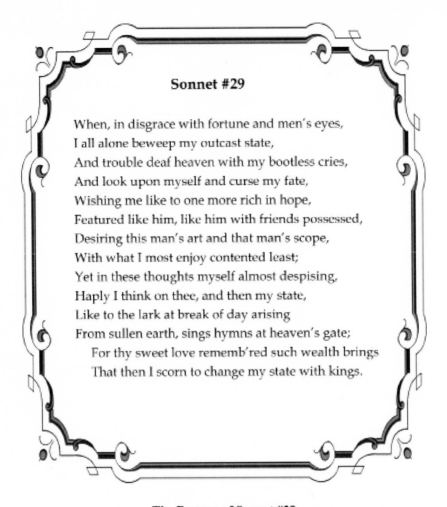

Sonnet #29

When, in disgrace with fortune and men's eyes,
I all alone beweep my outcast state,
And trouble deaf heaven with my bootless cries,
And look upon myself and curse my fate,
Wishing me like to one more rich in hope,
Featured like him, like him with friends possessed,
Desiring this man's art and that man's scope,
With what I most enjoy contented least;
Yet in these thoughts myself almost despising,
Haply I think on thee, and then my state,
Like to the lark at break of day arising
From sullen earth, sings hymns at heaven's gate;
　　For thy sweet love rememb'red such wealth brings
　　That then I scorn to change my state with kings.

The Essence of Sonnet #29

When my life seems so dismal that I begin to envy
others, I think of you and our love—and I realize that
I would not trade places with anyone.

To fully experience the sonnets visit www.sonnetsofshakespeare.com for a
live recording by Darrel Walters.

Diagram for Greater Understanding

1st Quatrain

        not getting on well   **luck**   **other people**
When, [in disgrace] with [fortune] and [men's eyes,]

        feel self-pity
I all alone [beweep my outcast state,]

        useless complaints
And trouble deaf heaven with my [bootless cries,]

And look upon myself and curse my fate,

2nd Quatrain

Wishing me like to one more rich in hope,

        good-looking   **having friends**
[Featured] like him, like him [with friends possessed,]

        skill   **insight**
Desiring this man's [art] and that man's [scope,]

With what I most enjoy contented least;

3rd Quatrain

Yet in these thoughts myself almost despising,

        by chance   **state of mind**
[Haply] I think on thee, and then my [state,]

Like to the lark at break of day arising

        gloomy
From [sullen] earth, sings hymns at heaven's gate;

Couplet

For thy sweet love rememb'red such wealth brings

        decline   **circumstance**
That then I [scorn] to change my [state] with kings.

SONNET 29

Description and Interpretation

In this masterful sonnet, considered among his best, Shakespeare reveals more than the usual amount of autobiographical material as he pours his heart out. In it he conveys a sense of failure, listing an account of shortcomings that he sees in himself relative to others. R. P. Blackmur calls this sonnet "a true monument of self-pity" (1962, 141). Considering the litany of personal weaknesses and insecurities that Shakespeare cites in the first two quatrains, Blackmur's assessment is not entirely without merit. Still, it seems a bit harsh.

Two factors need to be considered. First, best estimates tell us that Shakespeare wrote *The Sonnets* early in his career, at about age thirty. As a young, unestablished writer—his best-known plays yet to be written—he was understandably insecure. And second, he lived in a time when aspiring artists knew they had to ingratiate themselves to potential patrons by portraying themselves as humble and patrons as extraordinary. As Dennis Kay notes in *William Shakespeare: Sonnets and Poems*, Shakespeare was "acutely aware of the intense competition for the favor of patrons, grounding his hope in an intimacy that overrides other criteria" (1998, 132). His declarations of love and esteem for the young man to whom he wrote sprang from a mixture of genuine admiration and political acumen. Kay notes that, in several sonnets, "the discourses of love and clientage are inseparable" (1998, 132).

This sonnet is a companion of sorts to the one that follows it in the collection (Sonnet 30, 24). Each reveals regret, even despondency, but a fundamental difference puts Sonnet 30 under the category of Living Life's Span and Sonnet 29 under the category of Declaring Devotion. Many regrets cited in Sonnet 30 are for incidents not of Shakespeare's own making, reflecting the kind of battering that all of us take along life's journey. Sonnet 29 is more a matter of personal soul-searching, self-doubt, and jealousy, ending with an impassioned declaration of devotion to the recipient.

Exaggeration is alive and well here, as in so many of his sonnets. Probably the principal meaning of "in disgrace" is that he has been unlucky and is out of favor with people who could help him advance his career. By "beweep my outcast state" he may be reacting to a slowdown in employment more so than to personal attributes. The plague closed theaters for a while about that time, and exacerbating the problem was an attack by an established actor and playwright, Robert Greene, who labeled the young Shakespeare an "upstart crow" (Giroux 1982, 49). "Trouble deaf heaven with my bootless [useless] cries" may mean that he saw no relief from his troubles wherever he looked.

In the second quatrain, he begins to cite characteristics that he sees in others and covets for himself. He wants to be as good-looking as one person, have as many friends as another, and have the skill and insight of still others. Certainly he has pursuits that give him satisfaction, and personal traits that he feels good about, but he seems to have put himself into a funky mood: "with what I most enjoy contented least." The disenchantment he feels with himself, then, appears relative and temporary rather than absolute and enduring.

In the second line of the third quatrain, the sun comes out. He says that when he happens by chance (Haply) to think about the sonnet's recipient, his state of mind changes quickly and dramatically. He deftly compares that mental awakening to the characteristics of the lark, a ground-dwelling songbird that flies high and sings in flight:

> Haply I think on thee, and then my state,
> Like to the lark at break of day arising
> From sullen earth, sings hymns at heaven's gate.

After the word "arising," the unbroken movement between lines—a technique known as *enjambment*—thrusts the reader with momentum into an upward flight to heavenly thoughts. One can almost see a soaring, singing, jubilant lark and feel the presence of those blessed gates to heaven. What a wonderful ride that is into the crowning statement of the couplet:

> For thy sweet love rememb'red such wealth brings
> That then I scorn to change my state with kings.

The swing has been profound from the second quatrain, where he wanted to change places with almost anyone, to the couplet, where he rejects the thought of changing places with anyone, even a king. What a surge of joy these last four lines emit! It's a surge that effectively draws readers into Shakespeare's emotional state.

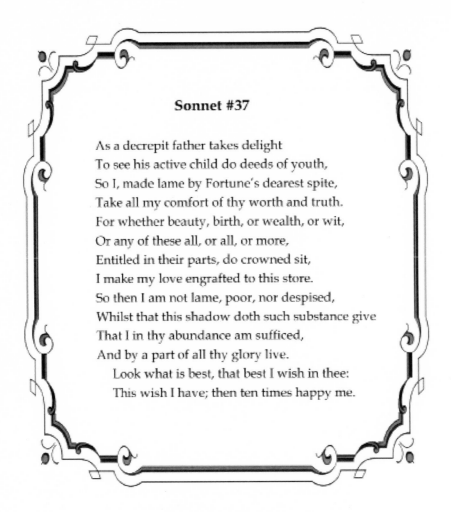

Sonnet #37

As a decrepit father takes delight
To see his active child do deeds of youth,
So I, made lame by Fortune's dearest spite,
Take all my comfort of thy worth and truth.
For whether beauty, birth, or wealth, or wit,
Or any of these all, or all, or more,
Entitled in their parts, do crowned sit,
I make my love engrafted to this store.
So then I am not lame, poor, nor despised,
Whilst that this shadow doth such substance give
That I in thy abundance am sufficed,
And by a part of all thy glory live.
    Look what is best, that best I wish in thee:
    This wish I have; then ten times happy me.

The Essence of Sonnet #37

Fortune has smiled on you, not me. I graft my life
to yours and live vicariously, all the while wishing
you well as a way of wishing myself well.

To fully experience the sonnets visit www.sonnetsofshakespeare.com for a live recording by Darrel Walters.

Diagram for Greater Understanding

1ˢᵗ Quatrain

father weakened by age
As a [decrepit father] takes delight

To see his active child do deeds of youth,

disabled **bad luck**
So I, [made lame] by [Fortune's dearest spite,]

lean on you
[Take all my comfort of thy worth and truth.]

2ⁿᵈ Quatrain

For whether beauty, birth, or wealth, or wit,

Or any of these all, or all, or more,

are among your attributes
[Entitled in their parts, do crowned sit,]

attached **accumulation**
I make my love [engrafted] to this [store.]

3ʳᵈ Quatrain

So then I am not lame, poor, nor despised,

you as my patron
Whilst that [this shadow] doth such substance give

have all I need
That I in thy abundance [am sufficed,]

And by a part of all thy glory live.

Couplet

consider your potential
[Look what is best,] that best I wish in thee:

(a reckless cliché?)
This wish I have; then [ten times] happy me.

SONNET 37

Description and Interpretation

Imagine Shakespeare facing two career needs simultaneously. One—seen repeatedly throughout these sonnets—is his need to flatter and stay in good standing with a young nobleman whom he genuinely admires, and who may be a source of patronage for his work. The other is the universal need for optimism—a need to believe that lying ahead are innumerable opportunities for successes and accomplishments.

Suppose that he begins to daydream one day in the early 1590s about the many, almost superhuman accomplishments he thinks are possible through his art if only someone of means were to become personally invested in his career. The first question he explores is whether he can convince a patron of his capabilities. He answers his own thoughts in short order: "No, I'd only sound like a braggart—like the 'upstart crow' that Robert Greene accused me of being. I'll have to find another tack."

Then suppose he hits upon the idea that, instead of promoting his own artistic capabilities, he should promote the overall capabilities of a potential patron. *You have so many outstanding qualities as compared to lowly me that my successes will depend upon my benefitting from all that you have to offer.* By flattering the patron into supporting his efforts, he will have a good chance of creating the successes he hopes for. Perverse as it sounds, casting himself as comparatively weak and unsuccessful may actually enable him to become strong and successful.

Now let's test that theory against the text of Sonnet 37. In the first quatrain, he portrays himself as lame due to misfortune, and taking comfort from the comparative strength of the sonnet's recipient, his young noble friend. He implies that his friend has beauty, birth, wealth, wit, and probably other wonderful attributes that might yet come to mind. He implies further that the friend's strengths are such that he, Will Shakespeare, takes strength from them by engrafting his love onto all that his friend has to offer. At this point, he has accomplished two things. First, he has flattered his friend with praise so beautiful that it may resound endlessly. Second, he has planted in his friend's mind the thought that sharing those bounteous advantages with Shakespeare is a natural act—almost a reasonable expectation.

Shakespeare then holds up before his friend a vivid picture of how much good that friend will have done. *Yes*, he admits, *the life I live will be but a shadow of your life, but from that shadow I will extract such substance as to make my life complete and productive.* His ultimate pitch will be to say

"I in thy abundance am sufficed,"
And by a part of all thy glory live.

"All thy glory." There's a phrase with the power to puff up anyone's ego! Further, Shakespeare's wish to be a part of that glory might easily be seen as complimentary more so than opportunistic.

Assuming that these conjectures account for the first of the two needs cited at the beginning of this writing—to flatter and stay in good standing with the young nobleman whom he genuinely admires—let us move to the second: belief that his reward for all the bowing and scraping will be innumerable accomplishments and successes. Unfortunately, Shakespeare's penchant for enthusiastic exaggeration confounds our attempts to deduce his most genuine thoughts. What might we make of the couplet?

Look what is best, that best I wish in thee:
This wish I have; then ten times happy me.

How much of that sentiment is sincere? Does Shakespeare genuinely wish for Herculean achievements from his young friend? Does he genuinely expect amazing advantages to accrue to him from the young friend's achievements? Does he see himself more as an appendage of one who succeeds than as one who succeeds by exercising his own abilities?

One clue might be found in "ten times." That sounds like a reckless cliché, tossed off more with emotion than with thought. And from what we can surmise of Shakespeare's sense of self—the confidence with which he pursued his work—he is not likely to have seen himself as an appendage of someone else. His accomplishments suggest an ego too large for him to "take all his comfort" from the accomplishments of another person. This sonnet sounds like a sea of hyperbole. Shakespeare seems to have cast a handful of seeds on what he sees as fallow ground with the hope that a grain or two would take root.

Sonnet #116

Let me not to the marriage of true minds
Admit impediments; love is not love
Which alters when it alteration finds,
Or bends with the remover to remove.
Oh no, it is an ever-fixed mark
That looks on tempests and is never shaken;
It is the star to every wandering bark,
Whose worth's unknown, although his height be taken.
Love's not Time's fool, though rosy lips and cheeks
Within his bending sickle's compass come;
Love alters not with his brief hours and weeks,
But bears it out even to the edge of doom.
   If this be error, and upon me proved,
   I never writ, nor no man ever loved.

The Essence of Sonnet #116

Hoping not to offend, I say that true love holds fast.
It withstands all changes and temptations over time—
even to the very end.

To fully experience the sonnets visit www.sonnetsofshakespeare.com for a live recording by Darrel Walters.

Diagram for Greater Understanding

steadfast
Let me not to the marriage of [true] minds

let in doubts
[Admit impediments;] love is not love

Which alters when it alteration finds,

weakens if the other person weakens
Or [bends with the remover to remove.]

unwavering point of light
Oh no, it is an [ever-fixed mark]

storms
That looks on [tempests] and is never shaken;

ship
It is the star to every wandering [bark,]

value is incalculable   **location is known**
Whose [worth's unknown,] although his [height be taken.]

love avoids Time's traps   **temptation**
[Love's not Time's fool,] though [rosy lips and cheeks]

reach
Within his [bending sickle's compass] come;

under Time's influence
Love alters not [with his brief hours and weeks,]

endures
But [bears it out] even to the edge of doom.

If this be error, and upon me proved,

I never writ, nor no man ever loved.

SONNET 116

Description and Interpretation

Sonnet 116 is generally acknowledged as one of the best, if not the best, of Shakespeare's collection. In it he tackles the unimaginably difficult task of defining love, and he does so by defining what love is not as well as what it is.

This piece may have been written to refute a position taken by the young man to whom Shakespeare was writing. Our current interest, though, is poetry—not biography. Poetic interests will be served best if we think of Sonnet 116 as a generic treatise, in sonnet form, on the nature of love.

This sonnet is straightforward and readily interpreted after the reader has gotten by the problematic opening: "Let me not to the marriage of true minds admit impediments." That feels almost like a disclaimer. *If you are someone who has found true love, I don't want to get in your way.*

The main event begins in the middle of the second line with the word "love" (how appropriate!). He is adamant that any relationship labeled "love," if it fails to hold fast in the face of alteration or removal, is an imposter. One's first thought may be that he is, in citing alteration or removal, referring solely to rejection by the other party. However, he could just as well be referring to alteration or removal by decay over time, or even by death. Thinking in those terms, one begins to see how highly idealistic this poem is—how high the standards are that he sets for love.

The second quatrain opens with an emphasis on the standards set down so earnestly in the first. "Oh no," he begins, reflecting back. *A relationship that cannot weather alteration or removal is not love.* Then he proceeds to say what love is by using a navigation metaphor.

it is an ever-fixed mark
That looks on tempests and is never shaken.

Love is like a star or a lighthouse—a guiding light that never wavers. Sailors called their guiding lights "marks." They knew they could look into the eye of a storm (tempest) and still find their way home safely so long as they had that "ever-fixed mark." As the sailor looks into the eye of the storm with assurance that his mark will help him prevail, so too those who share true love can look into the eye of life's storms with assurance that their love will help them prevail.

Elaborating on the metaphor, Shakespeare refers to love as "the star to every wandering bark" (sailing vessel). The sailors do not always know precise details about the mark they see. They can only calculate its height and location, and take comfort in knowing that it is there and it is steadfast. They can rely on it. Similarly, love is too great an entity to be confined to our knowing—to our understanding it fully. We can only take comfort in the knowledge that it is there, it is steadfast, and it is reliable.

In the third quatrain, Shakespeare returns to his favorite personified entity: Time. He gives to readers an image of the prototypical Father Time, wielding his ruinous sickle. Then he notes that love will not yield to temptations (rosy lips and cheeks) that are bound to reveal themselves within one's lifetime: "Love alters not with his brief hours and weeks." He casts love in terms of hours and weeks not to limit it, but to put it into perspective as compared to all of Time. Love ultimately looms large. It's not Time's fool. It will not let Time subdue it. And despite having a short span in literal terms, spiritually it will continue on and on, "even to the edge of doom."

Shakespeare's claims for the strength and staying power of love are extreme, but somehow they sound believable. Maybe the romantic spirit in us wants it to be true. Or maybe believability comes from his being a master of persuasion. He saves his final persuasive words for the couplet.

> If this be error, and upon me proved,
> I never writ, nor no man ever loved.

He has set the bar for love so high as to be ideal—unreachable. And yet he insists that he speaks the truth. He's so certain about his perception of love that he refuses to consider any view that contradicts his. *If error can be found in my contentions, and proven, I'll retract everything I've written about love. In fact, I'll consider love a mirage—a nonexistent entity that no one has ever experienced.*

Ne patulas blandis prebe Syrenibus aures,
Que dulci cantu sepe lepore nocent.

2.   D C

How oft, when thou, my music, music playst . . .
Do I envy those jacks that nimble leap
To kiss the tender inward of thy hand.

—from Sonnet 128

CHAPTER 5

Managing Relationships
Sonnets 128, 80, 109, 20, 115, 90, and 147

In this chapter's sonnets, Shakespeare describes feelings and experiences common in relationships yet today: infatuation (Sonnet 128), jealousy (Sonnet 80), guilt and apology (Sonnet 109), the nature of a relationship (Sonnet 20), the growth of a relationship (Sonnet 115), fear of loss (Sonnet 90), betrayal and regret (Sonnet 147).

Sonnets 128 and 147 are supposed to have been written to the dark lady. Sonnet 128 reveals Shakespeare's feelings about an early encounter, in which he finds the lady attractive as he watches her play a keyboard instrument. With the vignette taking place in 16th century England, the instrument would have been one from the harpsichord family. Sonnet 147 sits in stark contrast. In it he relates the extent to which their relationship—the nature of which is unknown today—has degenerated into a virtual sickness. Reading these two sonnets consecutively is an interesting exercise.

The four intervening sonnets in this section are supposed to have been written to Shakespeare's young friend of nobility. The accepted language and protocol between men at that time was such that many such sonnets could be read and enjoyed as if they had been written to a woman. Sonnet 80, for example, is treated here as if it were written to the young man—as most scholars have calculated that it was. If one were to claim that it was written to a woman, however, there is nothing in the sonnet itself that would refute that claim and much that would support it.

The extent to which the struggles and feelings revealed in these sonnets fit into the twenty-first century is uncanny. Technologies and opportunities change, but the most fundamental ingredients of a harmonious relationship remain constant.

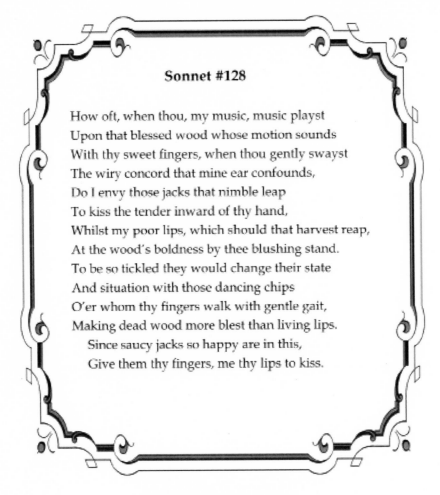

Sonnet #128

How oft, when thou, my music, music playst
Upon that blessed wood whose motion sounds
With thy sweet fingers, when thou gently swayst
The wiry concord that mine ear confounds,
Do I envy those jacks that nimble leap
To kiss the tender inward of thy hand,
Whilst my poor lips, which should that harvest reap,
At the wood's boldness by thee blushing stand.
To be so tickled they would change their state
And situation with those dancing chips
O'er whom thy fingers walk with gentle gait,
Making dead wood more blest than living lips.
 Since saucy jacks so happy are in this,
 Give them thy fingers, me thy lips to kiss.

The Essence of Sonnet #128

As you, my music, make music at the keyboard, I
envy those keys (jacks) the privilege of your touch.
I only wish that my poor lips were so blessed.

To fully experience the sonnets visit www.sonnetsofshakespeare.com for a live recording by Darrel Walters.

Diagram for Greater Understanding

often   **delight**
How [oft,] when thou, my [music,] music playst

those fortunate keys
Upon [that blessed wood] whose motion sounds

manipulate
With thy sweet fingers, when thou gently [swayst]

harmonies   **fails to absorb**
The [wiry concord] that mine ear [confounds,]

2nd Quatrain

keys
Do I envy those [jacks]that nimble leap

To kiss the tender inward of thy hand,

be doing the kissing
Whilst my poor lips, which should [that harvest reap,]

At the wood's boldness by thee blushing stand.

3rd Quatrain

my lips   **trade places**
To be so tickled [they] would [change their state

moving keys
And situation] with those [dancing chips]

over
[O'er] whom thy fingers walk with gentle gait,

Making dead wood more blest than living lips.

Couplet

those brash keys
Since [saucy jacks] so happy are in this,

Give them thy fingers, me thy lips to kiss.

SONNET 128

Description and Interpretation

In this playfully erotic sonnet, Shakespeare expresses his desire for a woman whom he sees playing a keyboard instrument. The instrument, not identified by name, almost certainly would have been a virginal (from the harpsichord family), supposedly named for its popularity among young ladies of sixteenth-century England. Noting Shakespeare's penchant for witty sexual innuendo, Stephen Booth surmises that his decision to use this popular keyboard instrument for Sonnet 128 "was probably in part dictated by the sexual potential in the name" (2000, 438). Shakespeare seemed to enjoy such playfulness.

The basic message is this: *When you play music at the keyboard, I don't take in the beauty of the sounds you're making. Rather, I become envious of the keys for the privilege they have of kissing your hand and enjoying the touch of your fingers.*

In the fun-with-words department, the word *music* occurs consecutively in the first line. Its first use is metaphorical, its second literal: "when thou, my music, music playst." Another piece of wordplay is Shakespeare's reference to the keys of the virginal as *wood*, then as *jacks*, and finally as *chips*. At no point does he refer to them directly with the word *keys*. By using the term *wood* he emphasizes that the keys are inanimate, and thus less worthy of attention than he. The term *chips* is a variant on the term *wood*—probably pressed into service because he needed a rhyme for *lips*.

He appears careless in using the term *jacks*, because the jacks are part of the instrument's internal mechanism. Such carelessness is not like him, however. Some (Booth 2000, 439; Jones 1997, 370) theorize that he used the errant term *jacks* purposely to capitalize on its other meaning in sixteenth-century England: a worthless, ill-bred man. That gives him an oblique way to hint again that he was more worthy of the lady's attention than were the keys.

In the first quatrain of this sonnet, Shakespeare leaves us hanging through three lines of subordinate material. Below is the first line of the first quatrain and the first line of the second quatrain welded together, with the intervening subordinate material squeezed out. Notice how logically those two lines fit together to deliver the main line of thought:

How oft, when thou, my music, music playst
Do I envy those jacks

The material omitted is the most difficult part of this sonnet to understand. By "blessed wood," Shakespeare means *fortunate wood; wood
having something that I desire*. By "gently swayst," he means not that the
woman was physically swaying, but rather that she was *gently controlling*
or *gently manipulating* the sound. He refers to the sound as a "wiry concord," because wires were being plucked, and *concord* is a synonym for
harmony. Finally, when he refers to that sound as something that "mine
ear confounds," he means something that his ear is not taking in and understanding—maybe because he is so distracted by the woman herself.

Now, let's return to the main event. The meat of this sonnet begins
in the second quatrain. He's envious of the keys that "nimble leap to
kiss the tender inward of thy hand." (In reality, the keys are more likely
to kiss the tips of her fingers. Maybe Shakespeare was more committed to writing a beautiful phrase than to being technically precise.) His
desire for the woman becomes plain when he says that his lips "should
that harvest reap," meaning it is they who should be doing the kissing.
Instead, they just stand there and blush.

As Shakespeare often does, he uses personification here to create a
willful person of a non-person—in this case, his lips. He says his lips
would gladly trade their living state for the dead state of the wood if
such a change would situate them to "be so tickled."

The delightful couplet brings to mind Vendler's (1997, 544) characterization of the piece as a "comic presentation of sexual jealousy."
In a bold surprise ending, Shakespeare offers to let the "saucy [brash]
jacks" revel in their good fortune and continue to kiss her fingers as
much as they want. "Give them thy fingers," he says in the last line,
and "me thy lips to kiss."

*So there. Let those keys—my rivals for your attention—play that bit
part all they want. I'll take the lead in this little drama, and kiss not
your fingers, but your lips.* Don't be surprised if you find the last line
of this sonnet difficult to read without smiling.

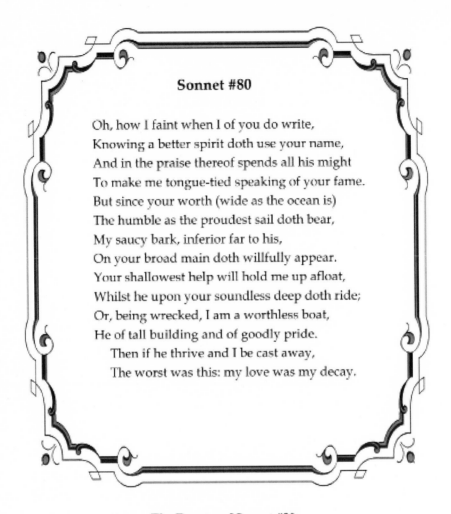

Sonnet #80

Oh, how I faint when I of you do write,
Knowing a better spirit doth use your name,
And in the praise thereof spends all his might
To make me tongue-tied speaking of your fame.
But since your worth (wide as the ocean is)
The humble as the proudest sail doth bear,
My saucy bark, inferior far to his,
On your broad main doth willfully appear.
Your shallowest help will hold me up afloat,
Whilst he upon your soundless deep doth ride;
Or, being wrecked, I am a worthless boat,
He of tall building and of goodly pride.
    Then if he thrive and I be cast away,
    The worst was this: my love was my decay.

The Essence of Sonnet #80

I feel inferior to another who pursues you. Still, I choose
to compete, and with encouragement from you I can win.
The risk I take is that acting on my love could bring
heartbreak.

To fully experience the sonnets visit www.sonnetsofshakespeare.com for a live recording by Darrel Walters.

Diagram for Greater Understanding

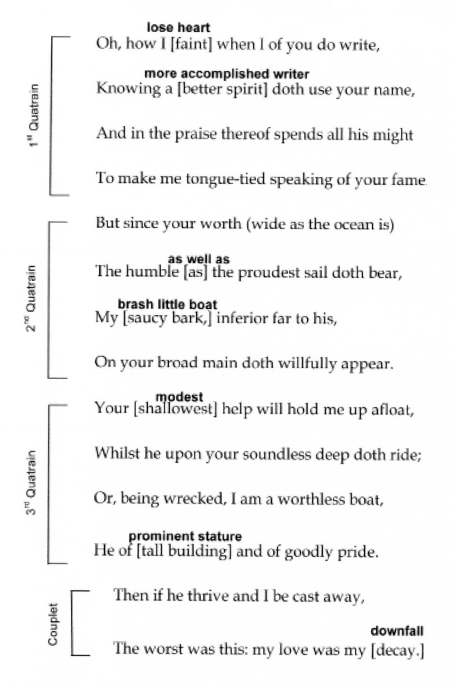

1ˢᵗ Quatrain

lose heart
Oh, how I [faint] when I of you do write,

more accomplished writer
Knowing a [better spirit] doth use your name,

And in the praise thereof spends all his might

To make me tongue-tied speaking of your fame.

2ⁿᵈ Quatrain

But since your worth (wide as the ocean is)

as well as
The humble [as] the proudest sail doth bear,

brash little boat
My [saucy bark,] inferior far to his,

On your broad main doth willfully appear.

3ᵈ Quatrain

modest
Your [shallowest] help will hold me up afloat,

Whilst he upon your soundless deep doth ride;

Or, being wrecked, I am a worthless boat,

prominent stature
He of [tall building] and of goodly pride.

Couplet

Then if he thrive and I be cast away,

downfall
The worst was this: my love was my [decay.]

SONNET 80

Description and Interpretation

The identity of a person known as the "rival poet" remains unknown. Perhaps a specific person, one of the star poets of late sixteenth-century England, was writing to the same young nobleman as Shakespeare. That poet's intent may have been to secure the status and patronage that Shakespeare coveted. Was there such a person, and did Shakespeare regard him as a "worthier pen" (Sonnet 79, not included in this book)? Or, since Shakespeare sometimes referred to the rival in plural, was the poet to whom he referred simply an imaginary amalgamation of several whom he saw as potential rivals?

Or there may have been no rival poet at all other than the one flowing from Shakespeare's pen—an invented figure lending drama to his work. And remember, as we read sonnets that scholars conjecture were written to the young man or the dark lady, another possibility is that many were written to no one in particular. Some may be pieces of art born of Shakespeare's imagination and his desire to see what he could make of it on paper.

In this sonnet, he casts the rival poet as a "better spirit," a superior writer whose presence and writing bothers Shakespeare greatly. "Oh how I faint," he says, meaning that he is disheartened to know that "a better spirit doth use your name." He implies that the rival poet's praise of the sonnet's recipient is sufficiently elegant and articulate to make him, Shakespeare, "tongue-tied."

Beginning in the second quatrain, another navigation metaphor unfolds. The young recipient of this poem becomes a great sea, open-minded (broad) enough to accept all kinds of sails. Not only is the grand sail of the Rival Poet present on the young friend's "broad main," but so will be the more humble sail of Shakespeare. His "saucy bark," he says, "doth willfully appear"—a brash little boat that refuses to be put off in the face of an outwardly more worthy rival. He will not accept the role of shrinking violet.

As overmatched as the "saucy bark" appears to be, a reader of that time may not have seen it so. Indelibly and proudly imprinted on the minds of all Englishmen of the time was the shellacking that the Spanish Armada's huge galleons had taken from England's comparatively small but more maneuverable ships in 1588. Shakespeare may actually have been hinting that history was on his side—that he had an excellent chance of coming out on top. Maybe his "saucy bark" would, as his country's small ships had, prevail over the more-imposing craft.

Shakespeare's fighting spirit in the face of the rivalry is notable here as compared to more fatalistic views that he expressed in sonnets preceding this one. Staying with the navigation metaphor, he plays on the conventional wisdom that small ships have an advantage in shallower waters. He appeals to his young friend to give him a break:

Your shallowest help will hold me up afloat,
Whilst he upon your soundless deep doth ride.

Suddenly he turns woefully negative in the middle of the third quatrain:

Or, being wrecked, I am a worthless boat,
He of tall building and of goodly pride.

Within that third quatrain, he confronts the two possible outcomes. He seems to be saying to the young friend to whom he has been writing for some time, *it's either him or me*. Realistically, though, Shakespeare is unlikely to have laid down an ultimatum to a young nobleman whose friendship and patronage he valued. More likely he was thinking aloud about possibilities, and about implications for him and his future. He may have written this sonnet as an appeal to the young man's sympathy and sense of fair play more so than as a challenge. That tone is apparent in the couplet:

Then if he thrive and I be cast away,
The worst was this: my love was my decay.

This couplet looks like an oh-woe-is-me psychological game. *I've been a close and loyal friend. Surely you wouldn't throw your influence to someone else and cast me away.* Then in the last line he does all he can to induce feelings of guilt and empathy. *My love and devotion to you has been all that you could ask. If I'm cast off despite that, the greatest pain would not be the actual loss of you as a friend and patron. The greatest loss would be the painful knowledge that my active pursuit of love and loyalty toward you appears to be the very thing that kept me from achieving it.*

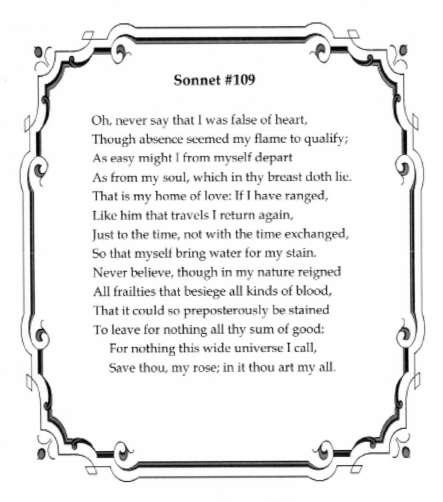

Sonnet #109

Oh, never say that I was false of heart,
Though absence seemed my flame to qualify;
As easy might I from myself depart
As from my soul, which in thy breast doth lie.
That is my home of love: If I have ranged,
Like him that travels I return again,
Just to the time, not with the time exchanged,
So that myself bring water for my stain.
Never believe, though in my nature reigned
All frailties that besiege all kinds of blood,
That it could so preposterously be stained
To leave for nothing all thy sum of good:
    For nothing this wide universe I call,
    Save thou, my rose; in it thou art my all.

The Essence of Sonnet #109

Despite my absence, I love you dearly and want to redeem
myself by picking up exactly where we left off. I suffer
weaknesses, but believe me when I say that you are my all.

To fully experience the sonnets visit www.sonnetsofshakespeare.com for a
live recording by Darrel Walters.

Diagram for Greater Understanding

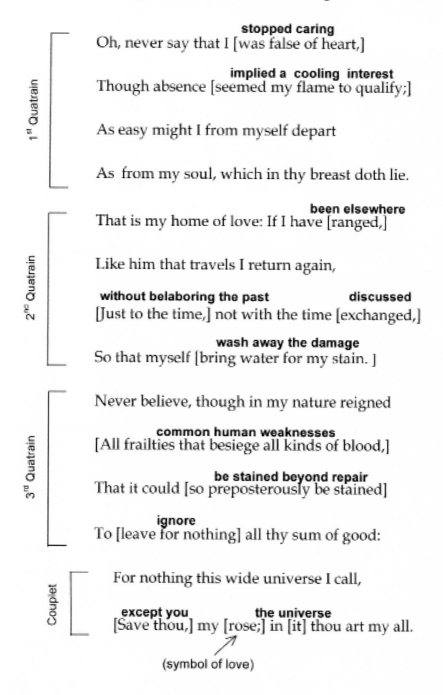

1ˢᵗ Quatrain

stopped caring
Oh, never say that I [was false of heart,]

implied a cooling interest
Though absence [seemed my flame to qualify;]

As easy might I from myself depart

As from my soul, which in thy breast doth lie.

2ᴺᴰ Quatrain

been elsewhere
That is my home of love: If I have [ranged,]

Like him that travels I return again,

without belaboring the past   **discussed**
[Just to the time,] not with the time [exchanged,]

wash away the damage
So that myself [bring water for my stain.]

3ᴿᴰ Quatrain

Never believe, though in my nature reigned

common human weaknesses
[All frailties that besiege all kinds of blood,]

be stained beyond repair
That it could [so preposterously be stained]

ignore
To [leave for nothing] all thy sum of good:

Couplet

For nothing this wide universe I call,

except you   **the universe**
[Save thou,] my [rose;] in [it] thou art my all.

(symbol of love)

SONNET 109

Description and Interpretation

Anyone who has lived to adulthood is almost certain to have made mistakes, affronted other people, felt regret over the mistakes and affronts, and suffered feelings of guilt. Following those human failings, as surely as spring follows winter, are pleas for forgiveness and attempts at atonement. It's all a matter of trying to manage relationships rather than let them disintegrate.

These are the experiences that Shakespeare seems to be going through in Sonnet 109. He may be answering charges of neglect initiated by his friend. Or he may be reacting to some troubling self-awareness. Either way, he approaches his friend with hat in hand.

He's writing after a period of absence. There is no way to know the nature or length of the absence he refers to. He may have just neglected to stay in touch for a period of time, or perhaps he had been on a prolonged tour with his acting company. All we can infer is that he had not seen the friend for a while, feared that his absence might damage their relationship, and was trying desperately to salve whatever wounds his absence had inflicted. He begins on the defensive, wanting to deny any thought his friend might have that he, Shakespeare, no longer cares for him as he once did.

Oh, never say that I was false of heart.

He must have realized immediately that his actions had left him on shaky ground—too much so for words to ease his friend's mind. He retreated, admitting that his friend did indeed have reason to look askance.

Though absence seemed my flame to qualify.

I realize that I'm not bursting with credibility right now. I've been neglectful. You have a right to wonder if the flame of our friendship that burns in me has been changed or lessened in some way during my period of absence. And then, to use the vernacular, he starts to "lay it on thick."

Shakespeare claims that his very soul lives within his friend's breast. "That is my home of love." He equates himself to the general traveler, who has to be on the road for a time but then returns, *as I have returned to you.* He emphasizes that he doesn't want to account for the intervening time—plow all that unpleasant ground. He seems to be saying, *Let bygones be bygones. I just want to pick up where we left off—wash away whatever stains I left on our relationship; expunge my bad record.*

Apparently unsure that he has sealed his case, and suspecting that his friend knows he's less than innocent, he makes a weak confession of sorts:

> Never believe, though in my nature reigned
> All frailties that besiege all kinds of blood,
> That it could so preposterously be stained
> To leave for nothing all thy sum of good.

It's the rather common but lame defense that says, *I'm only human. My nature is no less free of frailties than anyone else's.* It sounds as if he's admitting that he has been less considerate of his friend than he might have been. The extent of his human weaknesses is open to conjecture, ranging from simple neglect to—assuming a romantic relationship, which few Shakespeare scholars do—being unfaithful. He does want to be clear that the stains he left are too small, in his mind, to damage their relationship. He says that he could never "leave for nothing all thy sum of good."

This is one of the sonnets whose couplet is a major force. Shakespeare calls into play the entire universe. He says that from among all that exists, he applies the endearing name "my rose" to this sonnet's recipient alone. And furthermore, within that wide universe, "thou art my all."

My all? Shakespeare's life, even at this relatively early period, was certainly too rich for him to put all his eggs in that one proverbial basket. "Thou art my all" is clearly hyperbole. Finding himself in a tight situation of his own making, he's squirming and trying to rationalize his way out. In the sonnet that follows this one in the collection (not included in this book), he will go on to confess further and will make the audacious claim that the transgressions were good for him. *They taught me the value of our friendship.*

Some years later, Shakespeare would write *Hamlet.* A popular line from that play, invoked widely throughout the centuries when a person becomes overly defensive, might be appropriately paraphrased for Shakespeare in this setting. "The gentleman doth protest too much, methinks."

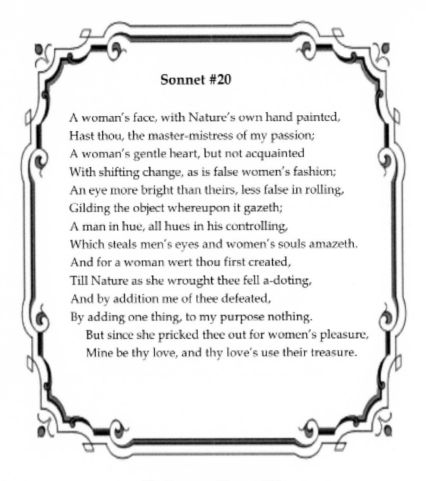

Sonnet #20

A woman's face, with Nature's own hand painted,
Hast thou, the master-mistress of my passion;
A woman's gentle heart, but not acquainted
With shifting change, as is false women's fashion;
An eye more bright than theirs, less false in rolling,
Gilding the object whereupon it gazeth;
A man in hue, all hues in his controlling,
Which steals men's eyes and women's souls amazeth.
And for a woman wert thou first created,
Till Nature as she wrought thee fell a-doting,
And by addition me of thee defeated,
By adding one thing, to my purpose nothing.
   But since she pricked thee out for women's pleasure,
   Mine be thy love, and thy love's use their treasure.

The Essence of Sonnet #20

Your beauty causes me to think that Nature intended you
initially for a woman, then changed her mind. So I can
only love you platonically, and leave the rest to women.

To fully experience the sonnets visit www.sonnetsofshakespeare.com for a
live recording by Darrel Walters.

Diagram for Greater Understanding

1st Quatrain

natural beauty
A woman's face, with [Nature's own hand painted,]

confusing object
Hast thou, the [master-mistress] of my passion;

A woman's gentle heart, but not acquainted

unreliability　　　　**fickle**　　　　**practice**
With [shifting change,] as is [false] women's [fashion;]

2nd Quatrain

straying
An eye more bright than theirs, less false in [rolling,]

enriching
[Gilding] the object whereupon it gazeth;

form　　**people**
A man in [hue,] all [hues] in his controlling,

attracts　　　　　　　　　　**excites**
Which [steals] men's eyes and women's souls [amazeth.]

3rd Quatrain

And for a woman wert thou first created,

created　　**became attracted**
Till Nature as she [wrought] thee [fell a-doting,]

locked me out
And by addition [me of thee defeated,]

a penis
By adding [one thing,] to my purpose nothing.

Couplet

selected you (sexual pun)
But since she [pricked thee out] for women's pleasure,

I'll love you as a friend　　**your sexual partners will be women**
[Mine be thy love,] and [thy love's use their treasure.]

SONNET 20

Description and Interpretation

This controversial and perplexing sonnet goes to the heart of speculation about whether Shakespeare was heterosexual or homosexual.
Today's trend toward live-and-let-live acceptance of sexual preference
probably lessens interest in the answer, and that may be best. A wide
range of opinions leads to nothing but greater uncertainty. Some cite
this sonnet as refutation of homosexuality (How clear can it get; he describes the man's maleness as "to my purpose nothing?"). Others cite it
as evidence of his homosexuality (he's obviously laying a smokescreen
to hide the fact that he's homosexual).

The end—the last six lines—may be the best place to start this
discussion. That takes us right to the heart of the matter. Shakespeare
explains the gentle, female-like loveliness of the young man's features
by creating a fantasy. In it, he says that the young man was originally
intended to be a woman. Then, implying that Nature is female (Mother
Nature), he conjectures that she became captivated by the loveliness of
the young woman she was creating. Nature then responded by "adding
one thing" to create a male. So Nature wanted the lovely young thing
for herself—as a male! We can only conclude, then, that Shakespeare
perceived Nature in terms of heterosexuality.

While Shakespeare's conjecture about Nature's role in this little
self-created fantasy may be a strong hint about his sexual orientation,
his next statements are much more than hints. Here is the very graphic
third quatrain in its entirety:

And for a woman wert thou first created,
Till Nature as she wrought thee fell a-doting,
And by addition me of thee defeated,
By adding one thing, to my purpose nothing.

So Nature's addition (the male sex organ) "me of thee defeated." *Any
designs I might have had for an intimate relationship with you due to
your extraordinary good looks and charm were defeated the day that
Nature decided to make you male.* Then to be forcibly clear about his
orientation, he refers to Nature's fantastic act as "adding one thing to
my purpose nothing."

Which argument should hold sway? Do Shakespeare's explicit state-ments show heterosexuality, or is his verbiage a smokescreen? Are we to take for face value the couplet, which says in essence, *since Nature made you a suitable companion for women, I can only love you as a friend, and leave the intimacy to them?* As convincing as this son-net sounds, the larger picture remains muddled. Probably the wisest course, as suggested in chapter 1, is to consider sexual orientation a non-issue. Sonnet 20 creates difficulty, but a neutral mindset may make the vast majority of the collection most enjoyable.

Shakespeare's love for the young man, here as much as anywhere, appears to be an "aesthetic affection." Patrick Cruttwell describes it as a remnant of the ancient Greek's "love of beauty, worship of noble birth, and an elegiac tenderness for youth" (1964, 48).

Innuendos about women in the first five lines of this sonnet contrast with that aesthetic affection for young men. Think for a moment about how men and women commonly segregate themselves into same-sex groups at social gatherings. Members of each group voice comrade-ship with members of their group and frustration with members of the other group. Shakespeare sounds as if he were note-taker in his group. Women are fickle ("false"), they change their minds ("acquainted with shifting change"), and they roll their eyes as if wanting to turn away from the man. *You are none of these things, yet you have many good qualities that I see in women*, says Shakespeare to the young man. It is that pull that he apparently finds frustrating, and that leads to his fantasy about Nature's stunt.

Before he ends the sonnet fantasizing about Nature's makeover, Shakespeare tries to describe the young man's allure. He acknowledges him as a male, "a man in hue" (usually meaning color, but in this gen-eral sense meaning simply "form"), and attributes to him the power to control all hues, man and woman. Men look at him and admire his ap-pearance (he "steals men's eyes"), and women's heart's beat faster in his presence ("women's souls amazeth"). Thus, Shakespeare dubs him "the master-mistress of my passion."

You have the fair looks and gentle spirit of a woman, but you lack those irritating female qualities. Therefore I am attracted to you. At the same time, though, I must face the reality of our platonic relationship.

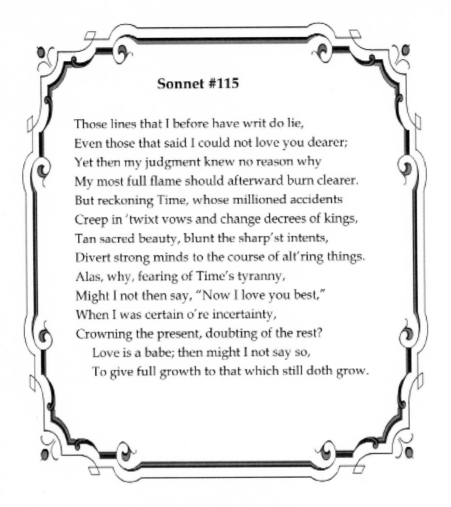

Sonnet #115

Those lines that I before have writ do lie,
Even those that said I could not love you dearer;
Yet then my judgment knew no reason why
My most full flame should afterward burn clearer.
But reckoning Time, whose millioned accidents
Creep in 'twixt vows and change decrees of kings,
Tan sacred beauty, blunt the sharp'st intents,
Divert strong minds to the course of alt'ring things.
Alas, why, fearing of Time's tyranny,
Might I not then say, "Now I love you best,"
When I was certain o're incertainty,
Crowning the present, doubting of the rest?
    Love is a babe; then might I not say so,
    To give full growth to that which still doth grow.

The Essence of Sonnet #115

Previous pledges that I loved you as fully as possible were
false. I was naïve then, and I dare not make the same mistake
again: time has taught me that love grows eternally

To fully experience the sonnets visit www.sonnetsofshakespeare.com for a
live recording by Darrel Walters.

Diagram for Greater Understanding

1ˢᵗ Quatrain

are in error
Those lines that I before have writ [do lie,]

Even those that said I could not love you dearer;

I was too immature to understand
Yet then [my judgment knew no reason why]

passion
My [most full flame] should afterward burn clearer.

2ⁿᵈ Quatrain

unpredictability
But reckoning Time, whose [millioned accidents]

Creep in 'twixt vows and change decrees of kings,

weather soft skin   impede intentions
[Tan sacred beauty,][blunt the sharp'st intents,]

accepting change
Divert strong minds to the course of [alt'ring things.]

3ʳᵈ Quatrain

Alas, why, fearing of Time's tyranny,

Might I not then say, "Now I love you best,"

over
When I was certain [o're] incertainty,

living for today
[Crowning the present, doubting of the rest?]

Couplet

perhaps I should acknowledge that
Love is a babe; then [might I not say so,]

put no restrictions on love
To [give full growth to that which still doth grow.]

SONNET 115

Description and Interpretation

Shakespeare uses the powerfully loaded word "lie" in the first line of this sonnet, but uses it as anyone might in saying off-handedly to a friend "I lied to you." The meaning: "I unintentionally told you something untrue a while ago, but now I've learned more. I'd like to set the record straight." *When I said earlier that I loved you as much as I could, I was immature in my judgment. I didn't realize then how much my feelings toward you would grow.*

Using "flame" to represent feelings of love, he doesn't claim that the flame is now bigger or brighter, but rather that it is clearer. The distinction is that his growth and maturity, and his improved powers of perception, have positioned him to see more clearly what had been there all the time.

The first quatrain offers no difficulties. The second does. Before delving into that second quatrain, read the sonnet without it. You'll see that quatrains 1, 3, and the couplet constitute a sensible and cohesive unit. What the second quatrain does, for all the difficulty it imposes, is to offer elaboration, strength, and body to the whole—once understood. (It also contributes to Shakespeare's writing a legitimate fourteen-line sonnet rather than a ten-line sonnet wannabe.)

In the opening of the second quatrain, "reckoning" could be an adjective describing Time (now a permanent proper noun in Shakespeare's vocabulary), or a verb form telling what Shakespeare did relative to Time. Let's assume the latter, that he "reckoned" Time, that is, took its effects into consideration in figuring out the progression of his feelings. He characterizes unpredictability as Time's "millioned accidents." (Now there is an interesting adjective!) Imagine all the vows sworn by people everywhere, and all the decrees made by kings who assume their wishes will be served. To describe the ubiquitous intrusion of Times "millioned" accidents into all those vows and decrees, he uses the delightful line "Creep in twixt vows and change decrees of kings."

So what havoc do Time's creeping accidents wreak? They

- "tan sacred beauty." Human beauty declines as classically soft skin becomes leathery from the sun and wind.
- "blunt the sharpest intents." Well-focused commitments, regardless of the zeal behind them, are blunted.

- "divert strong minds to the course of altering things." Minds set firmly on a particular course are induced to accept change.

Those observations pull Shakespeare back into a familiar theme in the third quatrain: fear of Time's tyranny. In his early sonnets, he rails against Time (see chapter 6 for a concentration of such sonnets). He repeatedly pictures it as the arch enemy of everything dear to him: "And nothing stands but for his scythe to mow" (Sonnet 60, p. 28). Habituated to thinking of Time as an enemy, he asks rhetorically why he should not continue to think that way.

> Alas, why, fearing of Time's tyranny,
> Might I not then say, "Now I love you best,"
> When I was certain o're incertainty,
> Crowning the present, doubting of the rest?

I know what Time is capable of. Now that I've awakened to the fact that my love for you has reached a new, higher level, wouldn't it be wise of me to latch onto that while I'm feeling so sure of myself? Shouldn't I grab what I have while I can, and not worry about tomorrow, with all its uncertainty?

The answer to his own question is a silent yet resounding "No." But why? Time is a powerful negative force. It destroys youthful beauty, decays all that humans hold dear, and eventually ravages all of nature's wonders. Shakespeare's new perspective, however, shows him that love is unlike—indeed opposite to—all that Time attacks so viciously.

Love is unique among all the entities of life. It does not decay with Time, but rather grows—nourished by the very hand that lays waste to all else. He will carry this revelation into Sonnet 116 (p. 88): "Love's not Time's fool." This pronouncement represents growth in Shakespeare's emotional maturity over the few years that he wrote these sonnets. Suddenly he feels a responsibility to set the record straight—to tell the world that Time does not destroy everything. Cupid's image as an infant should be taken seriously.

> Love is a babe; then might I not say so,
> To give full growth to that which still doth grow.

I regret having painted Time as black in all ways, and I'm pleased to acknowledge it as an instrument of growth for that most sacred entity: love.

Diagram for Greater Understanding

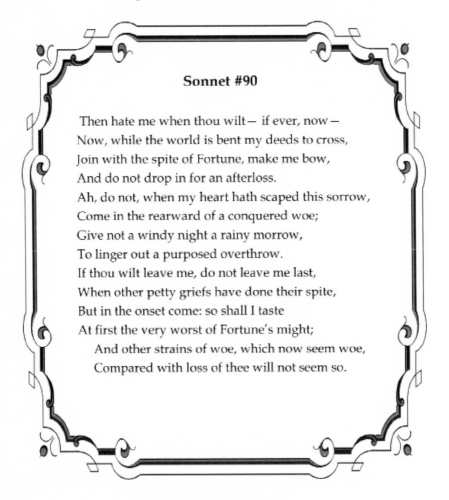

Sonnet #90

Then hate me when thou wilt— if ever, now—
Now, while the world is bent my deeds to cross,
Join with the spite of Fortune, make me bow,
And do not drop in for an afterloss.
Ah, do not, when my heart hath scaped this sorrow,
Come in the rearward of a conquered woe;
Give not a windy night a rainy morrow,
To linger out a purposed overthrow.
If thou wilt leave me, do not leave me last,
When other petty griefs have done their spite,
But in the onset come: so shall I taste
At first the very worst of Fortune's might;
    And other strains of woe, which now seem woe,
    Compared with loss of thee will not seem so.

The Essence of Sonnet #90

If you plan to reject me, do it now so my other woes—
rather than being crowned by disaster—will seem trivial
as compared to the loss of you.

To fully experience the sonnets visit www.sonnetsofshakespeare.com for a
live recording by Darrel Walters.

Diagram for Greater Understanding

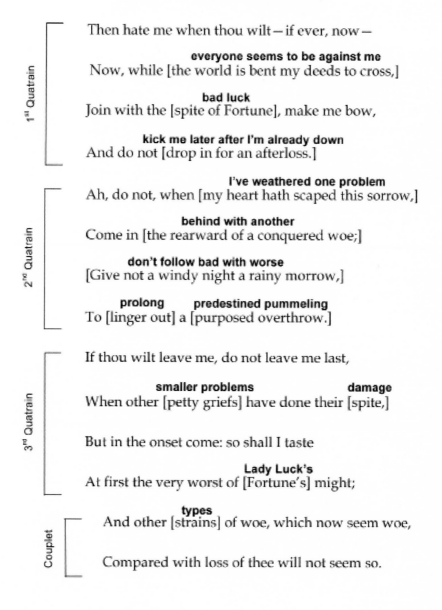

1ˢᵗ Quatrain

Then hate me when thou wilt—if ever, now—

everyone seems to be against me
Now, while [the world is bent my deeds to cross,]

bad luck
Join with the [spite of Fortune], make me bow,

kick me later after I'm already down
And do not [drop in for an afterloss.]

2ⁿᵈ Quatrain

I've weathered one problem
Ah, do not, when [my heart hath scaped this sorrow,]

behind with another
Come in [the rearward of a conquered woe;]

don't follow bad with worse
[Give not a windy night a rainy morrow,]

prolong   predestined pummeling
To [linger out] a [purposed overthrow.]

3ʳᵈ Quatrain

If thou wilt leave me, do not leave me last,

smaller problems   damage
When other [petty griefs] have done their [spite,]

But in the onset come: so shall I taste

Lady Luck's
At first the very worst of [Fortune's] might;

Couplet

types
And other [strains] of woe, which now seem woe,

Compared with loss of thee will not seem so.

SONNET 90

Description and Interpretation

We can only imagine the problems, worries, and indignities that Shakespeare might have suffered. Apparently he wrote this sonnet while feeling burdened on multiple fronts. "The world is bent my deeds to cross," he says. *Everywhere I look, it seems that people and institutions and events are out to get in my way and frustrate my efforts.* All active, productive people have those feelings at one time or another. Sometimes the cloud is innocuous and fleeting, sometimes severe and prolonged. Shakespeare, at the time of this writing, sounds as if he is stuck at the severe/prolonged end of the continuum.

At the top of his list of worries was an apparent fear of estrangement from the young man who had been a good friend, and perhaps patron, for some time. Over the course of several sonnets leading to this one, he spoke of his own shortcomings and of the young man's displeasure with him. All that angst leads logically to the first line of Sonnet 90:

Then hate me when thou wilt—if ever, now—

Why now? He goes on to explain that multiple forces are against him at the time—that Fortune (with the uppercase F now making a willful being of what we would call luck or fate) does not smile on him. *You may as well join the rest who are trying to bring me to my knees. Get in line.*

Now, while the world is bent my deeds to cross,
Join with the spite of Fortune, make me bow.

If the young man is to get in line, Shakespeare wants him at the front. He begs him to not "drop in for an after-loss"—kick him after he's already down. He pictures himself suffering through pain and sorrow from other problems that plague him, only to be blindsided afterward. He doesn't want the young man to "come in the rearward of a conquered woe." *Don't hit me from behind just as I recover from another problem and begin to feel that I'm in the clear.*

The colorful second half of the second quatrain makes his fears plain. He expects a loss of friendship with the young man to be a much more wrenching blow than the blows he might suffer before it arrives.

Give not a windy night a rainy morrow,
To linger out a purposed overthrow.

Don't take me from bad to worse. Don't enlarge and prolong my misery by following annoyance with devastation.

Then comes the bravado. He sounds like a man about to be executed, saying, "Throw away the blindfold. Forget the speeches. If that's what you're going to do, get on with it."

If thou wilt leave me, do not leave me last,
When other petty griefs have done their spite,
But in the onset come: so shall I taste
At first the very worst of Fortune's might.

This third quatrain is full of richness. "Do not leave me last" implores the young man to not make the worst of Shakespeare's losses an "afterloss." He elevates their relationship by referring to other losses as "petty griefs," and he implies a siege by using the powerful word "onset" rather than the pedestrian "start." By calling upon the comparatively remote sense of taste to represent the seat of his pain ("so shall I taste"), he implies that he will feel the loss of that friendship in every fiber of his being. The in-line rhyme, "at first the very worst," thrusts two extremes—first loss, greatest loss—into the reader's consciousness. And finally the two-word phrase, "Fortune's might" comes down like a hammer.

The two most salient messages of this sonnet are (1) Shakespeare is deeply concerned about the prospect of losing the friendship of the young man, and (2) he is, at the time of his writing this sonnet, beset by numerous other problems and worries that he wants the young man to know are present.

The couplet, rather than emphasizing either of those main themes, introduces a third: *your leaving me at the onset of my other problems will, in a perverse way, serve a purpose. You will cause all subsequent problems and losses to seem trivial by comparison.* Every dark cloud has a silver lining.

As "chin up" as that sounds, it may be more akin to the jilted lover who smiles and says through a stream of tears, "I'll be fine." The couplet only appears to salvage something from impending disaster. In reality, it offers more evidence that the loss of the young man's friendship would be devastating.

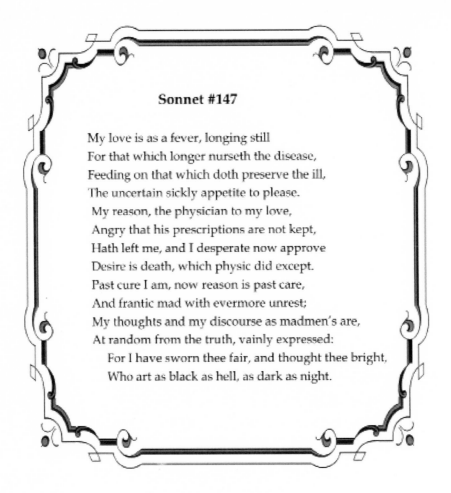

Sonnet #147

My love is as a fever, longing still
For that which longer nurseth the disease,
Feeding on that which doth preserve the ill,
The uncertain sickly appetite to please.
My reason, the physician to my love,
Angry that his prescriptions are not kept,
Hath left me, and I desperate now approve
Desire is death, which physic did except.
Past cure I am, now reason is past care,
And frantic mad with evermore unrest;
My thoughts and my discourse as madmen's are,
At random from the truth, vainly expressed:
    For I have sworn thee fair, and thought thee bright,
    Who art as black as hell, as dark as night.

The Essence of Sonnet #147

I am hopelessly entrapped by a passion that ignores
all reason and binds me to a lover who does me ill.

To fully experience the sonnets visit www.sonnetsofshakespeare.com for a live recording by Darrel Walters.

Diagram for Greater Understanding

1ˢᵗ Quatrain

ever
My love is as a fever, longing [still]

advances
For that which longer [nurseth] the disease,

Feeding on that which doth preserve the ill,

unpredictable
The [uncertain] sickly appetite to please.

2ⁿᵈ Quatrain

My reason, the physician to my love,

followed
Angry that his prescriptions are not [kept,]

hopeless   demonstrate
Hath left me, and I [desperate] now [approve]

physician   deny
Desire is death, which [physic] did [except.]

3ʳᵈ Quatrain

Past cure I am, now reason is past care,

And frantic mad with evermore unrest;

speech
My thoughts and my [discourse] as madmen's are,

varying   erroneously
[At random] from the truth, [vainly] expressed:

Couplet

lovely   radiant
For I have sworn thee [fair,] and thought thee [bright,]

Who art as black as hell, as dark as night.

SONNET 147

Description and Interpretation

This last sonnet of the chapter is not so much about managing a relationship as bemoaning a relationship that's become unmanageable. From the time the dark lady charmed the infatuated William Shakespeare at the keyboard (Sonnet 128, p. 94), their relationship gradually deteriorated until he came to loathe his passion for her, and ultimately to loathe her and himself.

Let's set up the metaphor that he uses here. Imagine a recalcitrant patient under the care of a physician who has made a diagnosis and given clear, concrete prescriptions. "You must avoid foods A, B, and C," says the physician, "and discontinue physical activities X, Y, and Z. These foods and activities are the cause of your ill health." The patient doesn't comply. He has an insatiable appetite for the forbidden foods and an obsessive craving for the forbidden activities.

As the illness progresses, the patient says to the physician, "These cravings of mine are going to kill me." The physician says "I disagree. You're thinking about this all wrong. It's not the cravings that are killing you. It's the bad foods and dangerous activities. Those cravings that you criticize are under your control. The real poison is something you've decided to impose on your body. Summon the willpower to follow my prescriptions and you'll be fine."

In the first quatrain of Sonnet 147, Shakespeare likens himself to just such a patient. He opens the sonnet by comparing his love to a persistent fever, hanging on because of his stubborn longing for the very thing that is making him sick. As he continues to pursue the forbidden fruit, he acknowledges that he's trying to satisfy what he calls an "uncertain sickly appetite."

The physician in this case is Shakespeare's own power of reason. His health is threatened by his relationship with the dark lady, a relationship fed by obsession. He knows better, and he tells himself so repeatedly—Dr. Reason at work. But his compulsion keeps him from heeding his own judgment.

My reason, the physician to my love,
Angry that his prescriptions are not kept,
Hath left me

I've ignored that which I know to be reasonable for so long that I finally have to admit something to myself: I've virtually lost my power of reason.

He then claims that his actions prove what he has contended all along. His obsession is doing him in: "Desire is death." Then he adds that his physician (power of reason) takes exception to that diagnosis. It's not the desire, but his inability to control that desire that's truly to blame.

Despondency sets in. He sees himself as having lost all chance of being cured. "Past cure I am." And furthermore, his "physician" no longer seems to care about what happens. "Now reason is past care." Is he ready to accept the hold that this woman has on him, and continue with his destructive behavior?

Maybe not. Often when a person invokes the words "I don't care," the merry-go-round continues to spin in that person's head. That would make a lie of "reason is past care." He says that his reason is "frantic mad with evermore unrest." Apparently his mind is still running through his problems at high speed. He makes no sense, either in his thoughts or his speech. He knows that he's been lying to himself and expressing himself in falsehoods:

My thoughts and my discourse as madmen's are,
At random from the truth, vainly expressed.

All this angst leads to perhaps the most startling couplet in all the sonnets. He puts on paper the terrible, troubling chasm between what he has thought the dark lady to be (and claimed her to be) and what he has found her to be in reality. He shifts quickly to direct address, as if she were there:

For I have sworn thee fair, and thought thee bright,
Who art as black as hell, as dark as night.

This couplet is as functional as it is shocking. It certainly explains the pain and suffering that he portrayed in the body of the sonnet. Also, it is so blatantly direct that C. L. Barber, in "An Essay on Shakespeare's Sonnets," wonders if the dark lady ever saw it. "These are outrageous poems: one wonders whether in fact most of them can have been sent to the poor woman—whether many of them were not offstage exercises in hate and despite [sic] written from a need to get something out of the poet's system" (1987, 21).

When wasteful war shall statues overturn,
And broils root out the work of masonry,
Nor Mars his sword nor war's quick fire shall burn
The living record of your memory.

—from Sonnet 55

Source: Philadelphia Museum of Art
Access Number: 1985–52–12872
Title: The Shepherds
Source: Dutch, Aelbert Meyeringh
Date: 1695

CHAPTER 6

Keeping Beauty Alive
Sonnets 15, 55, 54, 17, 65, and 18

Two of Shakespeare's obsessions were time and beauty. As seen in previous chapters, he often referred to Time—a proper noun representing a willful being who wreaked havoc on everyone and everything. In this chapter, Time debates with Decay (another willful being) to plot the fate of the young man to whom Shakespeare writes (Sonnet 15). Time also turns monuments and buildings to rubble (Sonnet 55), sends lives that lack character into oblivion (Sonnet 54), threatens to blunt the effects of Shakespeare's writing (Sonnet 17), and steals beauty from the young (Sonnet 65, among many). Ironically, in one of his early sonnets (Sonnet 18) Shakespeare claimed to have conquered the ravages of Time. Though among his most revered, Sonnet 18 apparently signals that considerable insight and maturation lay ahead for the young poet.

"So long lives this, and this gives life to thee" (Sonnet 18) was the bravado of a young writer who would wrestle with the demon Time his whole life. In later sonnets he bemoaned much that he had lost to Time (Sonnet 30, p. 24), regretted his poor management of time (Sonnet 109, p. 102), and—in defiance of Time's penchant for challenging love—challenged Time in return with "Love's not Time's fool" (Sonnet 116, p. 88). Through it all, he never seemed to lose faith in the thought that he could soften the deleterious effects of Time by preserving on paper some of the people and places that Time despoiled.

In trying to save beauty from Time's wrecking ball, Shakespeare created one of history's most enduring lines. Countless millions are familiar with the question that opens Sonnet 18: "Shall I compare thee to a summer's day?"

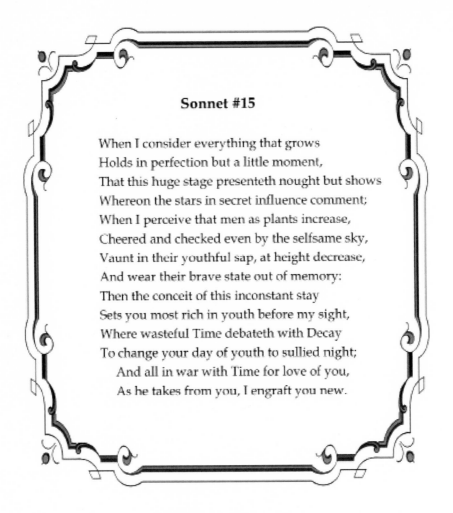

Sonnet #15

When I consider everything that grows
Holds in perfection but a little moment,
That this huge stage presenteth nought but shows
Whereon the stars in secret influence comment;
When I perceive that men as plants increase,
Cheered and checked even by the selfsame sky,
Vaunt in their youthful sap, at height decrease,
And wear their brave state out of memory:
Then the conceit of this inconstant stay
Sets you most rich in youth before my sight,
Where wasteful Time debateth with Decay
To change your day of youth to sullied night;
    And all in war with Time for love of you,
    As he takes from you, I engraft you new.

The Essence of Sonnet #15

Knowing the impermanence of youth—and of life itself—
I declare war on Time for your sake, and restore to you in
my verse what he takes from you by decay.

To fully experience the sonnets visit www.sonnetsofshakespeare.com for a live recording by Darrel Walters.

When I consider everything that grows

Holds in perfection but a little moment,

life **is but a series of impressions**
That [this huge stage] [presenteth nought but shows]

fate **without warning** **has a say**
Whereon [the stars] [in secret] [influence comment;]

grow
When I perceive that men as plants [increase,]

encouraged, then stopped **same conditions**
[Cheered and checked] even by the [selfsame sky,]

boast **begin to degenerate**
[Vaunt] in their youthful sap, at height [decrease,]

live with bravado until dead and forgotten
And [wear their brave state out of memory:]

realization **unstable life**
Then the [conceit] of this [inconstant stay]

Sets you most rich in youth before my sight,

ruinous **discusses respective roles**
Where [wasteful] Time [debateth] with Decay

impure
To change your day of youth to [sullied] night;

And all in war with Time for love of you,

immortalize you
As he takes from you, I [engraft you new.]

(margin labels: 2nd Quatrain; 3rd Quatrain; Couplet)

SONNET 15

Description and Interpretation

The body of Sonnet 15, up to the couplet, is a vivid reminder of our mortality. As obvious as the truth of mortality is, we never seem to tire of hearing or thinking about it, as reflected in plays and movies that we find entertaining. So Shakespeare has a hot topic here—one he will tap frequently in other sonnets and in his plays. All that fascination over mortality woven into elegant poetry makes the first twelve lines of this sonnet spellbinding. Already in the first two lines he forces readers to look mortality squarely in the eye:

> everything that grows
> Holds in perfection but a little moment.

Throughout the first two quatrains, this sonnet could apply to anyone. It is universal and philosophical, with the world cast as a huge stage (not the only time Shakespeare would do that). He observes that the stars (fate) have a major behind-the-scenes say in what happens to all of us:

> this huge stage presenteth nought but shows
> Whereon the stars in secret influence comment.

As if "holds in perfection but a little moment" is not humbling enough, he lumps humans with animals and plants as a general category of things that grow. He says that all growing things are "cheered and checked even by the selfsame sky": all are encouraged onward (cheered), and all are stopped (checked) by conditions of nature when the time comes—conditions symbolized by the sky that overlooks everything..

Particularly ominous is the statement that people must—after rounding the height of youthful vigor and descending into a less ideal physical state—"wear their brave state out of memory." For the remainder of life, they muddle along in a state of bravery and false bravado, and ultimately disappear from all memory. Another 350 years would pass before actress Bette Davis offered a similar take on life with her famous quip, "Old age ain't no place for sissies."

Seeing the ravages of Time in contrast to the youthful beauty and vigor of the young man to whom he is writing, Shakespeare makes the transition from general observation to personal commentary:

> Then the conceit of this inconstant stay
> Sets you most rich in youth before my sight.

The fate to be suffered by all when they enter that dismal state of non-youth causes me to appreciate all the more the youthful state that I see in you.

Shakespeare remains personal as he turns to the subject of the young man's mortality: "Time debateth with Decay to change your day of youth to sullied night." He is picturing Time and Decay as two willful entities having an imaginary conversation about their roles in the ultimate ruination of the young man. As helpless as everyone seems to be to do anything about the impending danger of growing old, Shakespeare vows action. He will preserve the young man's youth in his verse:

> And all in war with Time for love of you,
> As he takes from you, I engraft you new.

By "engraft" he means to plant firmly (i.e., immortalize)—the first of many times in these sonnets that he will say *through my writing you will live on.* The most famous such pledge is in the couplet of Sonnet 18 (p. 144).

A major difference between this sonnet and Sonnet 18 is that the principal message here—the endpoint—is not his pledge to preserve the young man's youth in verse. You might ask, "How can that be? He makes that proclamation in the couplet, and there's nowhere to go from there."

There is someplace to go: to Sonnet 16 (not included in this book). Sonnets 15 and 16 are similar in technique to Sonnets 73 and 74 (pp. 32 and 36): they constitute what might be thought of as a double sonnet. In both cases, the second of the pair (Sonnets 74 and 16) begins with the word "But." In Sonnet 16, we see that the couplet of Sonnet 15 was the midpoint of Shakespeare's message. He is still in the mode of the procreation sonnets. He goes on to say in Sonnet 16, "Fortify yourself in your decay." *I'll confront your mortality in verse, but you do your part by fathering a child. That child's presence will keep part of you alive.*

The purpose of this book, besides clarifying some of the sonnets, is to help you study and interpret others more readily. You might study Sonnet 16 as a sequel to this one, and Sonnet 12 for its similar form and content.

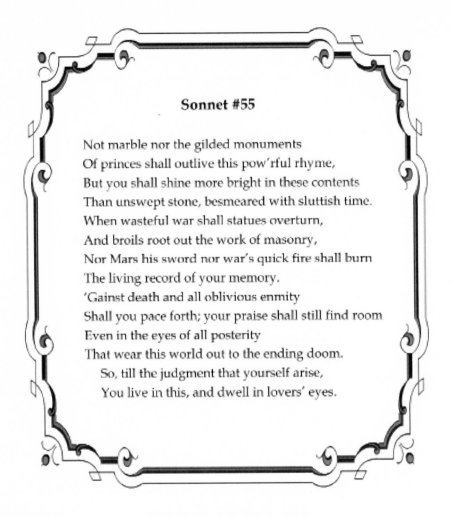

Sonnet #55

Not marble nor the gilded monuments
Of princes shall outlive this pow'rful rhyme,
But you shall shine more bright in these contents
Than unswept stone, besmeared with sluttish time.
When wasteful war shall statues overturn,
And broils root out the work of masonry,
Nor Mars his sword nor war's quick fire shall burn
The living record of your memory.
'Gainst death and all oblivious enmity
Shall you pace forth; your praise shall still find room
Even in the eyes of all posterity
That wear this world out to the ending doom.
   So, till the judgment that yourself arise,
   You live in this, and dwell in lovers' eyes.

The Essence of Sonnet #55

Your memory will outlive the structures of civilization.
While war and pestilence wear them down, you will live
in this verse for all time and inspire lovers who read it.

To fully experience the sonnets visit www.sonnetsofshakespeare.com for a
live recording by Darrel Walters.

Diagram for Greater Understanding

gold-adorned
Not marble nor the [gilded] monuments

Of princes shall outlive this pow'rful rhyme,
           what I say here
But you shall shine more bright in [these contents]

    neglected structures   **eventually made filthy**
Than [unswept stone,] [besmeared with sluttish time.]

        turn the world upside down
When wasteful war shall [statues overturn,]

1st Quatrain

    violent conflicts   **tear down buildings**
And [broils] [root out the work of masonry,]

  neither the weapons of war
[Nor Mars his sword] nor war's quick fire shall burn

    what I have written about you
[The living record of your memory.]

2nd Quatrain

      blind malice
'Gainst death and all [oblivious enmity]

        you will be revered
Shall you pace forth; [your praise shall still find room]

Even in the eyes of all posterity

        end of human existence
That wear this world out to the [ending doom.]

3rd Quatrain

    Judgment Day   **when you ascend to**
So, till the [judgment] [that yourself arise,]

    inspire lovers who read about you
You live in this, and dwell in lovers' eyes.

Couplet

SONNET 55

Description and Interpretation

This sonnet reads like an ode to the power of poetry. Shakespeare begins by citing objects generally expected to defy the ravages of Time: marble, with all its density and strength, and gold-laden monuments belonging to royalty. None of them, he says, will outlive "this powerful rhyme." His confidence soars, a stark contrast to "wishing me like to one more rich in hope" (Sonnet 29, p. 80), "with old woes new wail my dear time's waste" (Sonnet 30, p. 24), and "made lame by Fortune's dearest spite" (Sonnet 37, p. 84). He says here, "You shall shine more bright in these contents." *I am doing all I can to help you become immortal, and I will succeed.*

Shakespeare implies that he is, through his writing, caring for the young man in ways that the world at large is not cared for. He describes the marble and monuments as "unswept"—neglected. Those objects, he says, will be overwhelmed by "sluttish time." Here he does not use the uppercase T. He's not writing of "Time," the active, willful miscreant who mows us down with his scythe. Rather, he's writing about "time," the passive entity that simply passes by while tangible objects become nasty and filthy for lack of care. He paints a vivid image, with the graphic word "besmeared" suggesting that everything worldly will become coated with unimaginable dirt.

The second quatrain is a word-picture of human chaos, past and projected. He describes war as "wasteful war" because of all that is destroyed and lost forever. Statues represent the countless manmade objects that will be upended in the carnage. By "broils" he means raging conflicts and all the violence and destruction they bring with them. The phrase "root out the work of masonry" paints a dramatic picture of conflict tearing down buildings that devoted masons had erected years earlier. He says that in contrast to this powerful poem—a literary monument—the physical monuments of this world will not endure indefinitely.

As he so commonly does, Shakespeare makes a transition from general observations to specific prognostications. Neither Mars himself (the god of war) nor the fires that erupt in the midst of war "shall burn the living record of your memory" (unless someone leaves the only copies of Sonnet 55 in the wrong place, a detail not allowed to dampen the spirit of a romantic).

So Shakespeare has set the young man to whom he writes on a path to immortality. As J. W. Lever characterizes the message of Sonnet 55, "Here the hostile forces of existence are assembled and total victory over their massed forces is proclaimed" (1956, 270).

By "oblivious enmity" in the first line of the third quatrain, Shakespeare is referring to any and all destructive forces, including those initiated by persons having no relationship with—in fact, no knowledge of—the young man to whom he writes. Oblivious enmity is pure blind malice, people perpetrating violent acts on others, without any sense whatsoever of the fallout that might ensue. Such fallout in today's language of war is commonly referred to as "collateral damage." Shakespeare is telling the young man that he will be safe not only from direct attack, but also from collateral damage.

So now the young man can be confident that no matter how many centuries pass, all posterity will find room in its reading and its discourse for praise of him. To make clear that he's referring literally to "forever," Shakespeare describes future praise as coming from "all posterity that wear this world out to the ending doom."

"Doom" has the specific meaning of "Doomsday"—the term that signifies the end of the world as we know it. He ties praise of the young man not only to posterity but also to the Almighty when he writes, "Till the judgment that yourself arise." According to the Bible, all worthy souls shall ascend to heaven on Judgment Day. Shakespeare has been so audacious as to imply that the young man will be one of those souls.

Some maintain that Shakespeare wrote all of his sonnets to specific persons for specific purposes, and without an eye to promoting his own artistry beyond his lifetime. The last line of this sonnet suggests otherwise. *Until Judgment Day*, he says, *you live in this poem and in the eyes of lovers*. He seems to relish having left something for posterity as an inspiration to lovers yet unborn, an indication that he likely wrote this, and perhaps other sonnets, to be read and appreciated for generations to come.

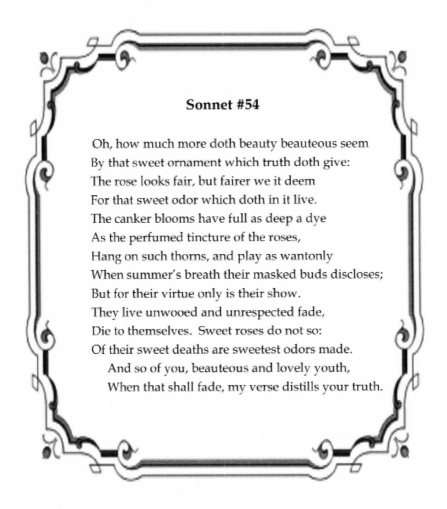

Sonnet #54

Oh, how much more doth beauty beauteous seem
By that sweet ornament which truth doth give:
The rose looks fair, but fairer we it deem
For that sweet odor which doth in it live.
The canker blooms have full as deep a dye
As the perfumed tincture of the roses,
Hang on such thorns, and play as wantonly
When summer's breath their masked buds discloses;
But for their virtue only is their show.
They live unwooed and unrespected fade,
Die to themselves. Sweet roses do not so:
Of their sweet deaths are sweetest odors made.
    And so of you, beauteous and lovely youth,
    When that shall fade, my verse distills your truth.

The Essence of Sonnet #54

As fragrance enhances the beauty of a rose, and leaves
behind perfume, so truth enhances the beauty of a person,
and leaves behind reputation. My verse preserves yours.

To fully experience the sonnets visit www.sonnetsofshakespeare.com for a live recording by Darrel Walters.

Diagram for Greater Understanding

1st Quatrain

Oh, how much more doth beauty beauteous seem

internal value
By that sweet ornament which [truth] doth give:

cultivated rose **lovely** **judge**
The [rose] looks [fair,] but fairer we it [deem]

fragrance
For that [sweet odor] which doth in it live.

2nd Quatrain

wild roses **rich a color**
The [canker blooms] have full as [deep a dye]

pigment
As the perfumed [tincture] of the roses,

unrestrained
Hang on such thorns, and play as [wantonly]

breeze **exposes their hidden buds**
When summer's [breath] [their masked buds discloses;]

3rd Quatrain

their only admirable quality is their appearance
But [for their virtue only is their show.]

not sought out
They live [unwooed] and unrespected fade,

Die to themselves. Sweet roses do not so:

perfumes
Of their sweet deaths are [sweetest odors] made.

Couplet

And so of you, beauteous and lovely youth,

encapsulates your worth
When that shall fade, my verse [distills your truth.]

SONNET 54

Description and Interpretation

The wild rose and the cultivated rose, Shakespeare says in this sonnet, are both beautiful to see. Their exteriors are comparable in color and richness, they hang on similar thorn-filled vines, and they bob in the summer breeze (described imaginatively as summer's breath)—showing off their blossoms for all to see. The important difference is that the cultivated rose has within it a fragrance that adds immeasurably to its appeal. The wild rose lacks that fragrance, and so is able to offer only the virtue of its lovely appearance.

Near the end of the sonnet, you will see that Shakespeare has set himself up to compare two kinds of people. As with the roses, the exteriors of the two kinds of people are comparable. The important difference is that one has a valuable inner quality analogous to the fragrance of the cultivated rose, a quality that adds immeasurably to that person's appeal.

Rather than launch immediately into the analogy, Shakespeare opens the sonnet with a general observation.

> Oh, how much more doth beauty beauteous seem
> By that sweet ornament which truth doth give.

That which is beautiful is made even more beautiful by the presence of truth. He leaves the specific nature of "truth" hanging undefined and then launches into a comparison of the two kinds of roses—a comparison that dominates the remainder of the sonnet all the way to the couplet. Only as he begins the couplet with the words "And so of you" does Shakespeare reveal his intent to compare the recipient of the sonnet to the cultivated rose. And only with the last word of the sonnet does he return to the key term from the powerful opening statement: "truth." With that last word, the reader realizes that the "sweet ornament" referred to early in the sonnet, labeled "truth" by Shakespeare, is a desirable human attribute that today we would most likely label *character*. And only then does the analogy of people (hollow versus principled) to flowers (unscented versus fragrant) strike with full force.

The greater attractiveness of the fragrant rose (and by extension, the principled person) during its lifetime is only part of the analogy, and not the most salient part. An even more powerful contention within Shakespeare's extensive comparison of the two kinds of roses is that the inner fragrance of the cultivated rose enables its influence to linger even after it has died. How? The fragrance of the rose is distills into perfume, enabling it to be valued and enjoyed by others indefinitely. Wild roses, in contrast, will live their lives "unrespected" and then "die to themselves."

After the reader has digested those powerful thoughts about the rose's influence beyond death, Shakespeare, in the couplet, attaches parallel thoughts to the sonnet's recipient: "my verse distils your truth." *As the cultivated rose's superiority over the wild rose shines indefinitely because its fragrance is distilled within perfume, so will your superiority over lesser persons shine indefinitely because your inner qualities will be distilled within my verse.*

J. W. Lever interprets the "masked buds" of the canker blooms (wild roses) as a sensual reference to "the ladies of fashion whose masks [veils] are a mere show of virtue intended to stimulate desire" (1956, 213). In other words, Lever conjectured that Shakespeare was contrasting the disingenuous, veiled women of the time with the highly principled recipient of this sonnet.

Two terms that Shakespeare uses in this sonnet are particularly interesting. General practice today is to use the term *fragrance* to denote a pleasant smell and *odor* to denote an unpleasant smell. The term *fragrance*, however, did not come into common use until about half a century after Shakespeare's death. He was quick to invent new words when he felt the need—as many as 1,700, most in use yet today (Lederer 1991, 93)—but here he made the most of the available vocabulary. In writing about what we would refer to as the "fragrance" of the cultivated rose, he turns the term "odor" positive by labeling it a "sweet odor."

Further, he never uses the terms "cultivated rose" or "wild rose" while comparing the two. Rather, he plays one of the word games for which he is notorious. In his day, a canker sore was referred to derisively as a wild rose to emphasize its appearance as an out-of-control red blossom on the lip. He turns that word play on itself by referring to wild roses as "canker blooms." That, in turn, frees him to refer to the cultivated rose as simply a "rose."

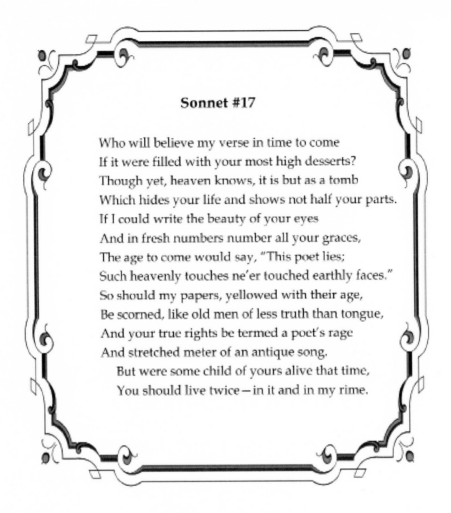

Sonnet #17

Who will believe my verse in time to come
If it were filled with your most high desserts?
Though yet, heaven knows, it is but as a tomb
Which hides your life and shows not half your parts.
If I could write the beauty of your eyes
And in fresh numbers number all your graces,
The age to come would say, "This poet lies;
Such heavenly touches ne'er touched earthly faces."
So should my papers, yellowed with their age,
Be scorned, like old men of less truth than tongue,
And your true rights be termed a poet's rage
And stretched meter of an antique song.
    But were some child of yours alive that time,
    You should live twice — in it and in my rime.

The Essence of Sonnet #17

If I were to write fully and honestly of your qualities, the
next generation would not believe me—unless a beautiful
child of yours were alive to lend credibility to my verse.

To fully experience the sonnets visit www.sonnetsofshakespeare.com for a
live recording by Darrel Walters.

Sonnet #17: Diagram for Greater Understanding

1st Quatrain

Who will believe my verse in time to come

finest qualities
If it were filled with your [most high desserts?]

Though yet, heaven knows, it is but as a tomb

virtues
Which hides your life and shows not half your [parts.]

2nd Quatrain

If I could write the beauty of your eyes

lines   **declare**
And in fresh [numbers] [number] all your graces,

The age to come would say, "This poet lies;

Such heavenly touches ne'er touched earthly faces."

3rd Quatrain

So should my papers, yellowed with their age,

rejected as false   **who talk much, but can't be believed**
Be [scorned,] like old men [of less truth than tongue,]

valid praise   **irrational ranting**
And your [true rights] be termed a poet's [rage]

exaggerated poetry
And [stretched meter of an antique song].

SONNET 17

Description and Interpretation

As noted earlier, in the description on page 14, the first seventeen sonnets are commonly called the "procreation sonnets" for Shakespeare's effort to convince the young man to preserve his beauty by having a child. Some scholars refer to them as the "marriage sonnets," but that label is less apt. As J. W. Lever observes in *The Elizabethan Love Sonnet*,

> Nowhere in the group does he concern himself with the character of the wife the friend might choose, or spare a thought for her qualifications in the way of beauty or virtue. . . . The end of marriage is simply and solely procreation. (1956, 189)

Shakespeare harps on two themes having to do with preservation of the young man's beauty: a child from the young man's genes, and verses from Shakespeare's pen. In this sonnet he offers overt and immediate speculation about the future effects of his writing.

> Who will believe my verse in time to come
> If it were filled with your most high desserts?

In Sonnet 15 (p. 124), he said that his verse would help keep the memory of the young man alive after Time and Decay had their way, *but now I'm not so sure*, he says. *Your wonders are so extreme as to be doubted no matter what I say.*

In a typical show of exaggerated humility, he then hastens to add

> Though yet, heaven knows, it [my verse] is but as a tomb
> Which hides your life and shows not half your parts.

Casting his writing as a "tomb" elevates the young man by comparison: *my poetry is so inadequate to the job of perpetuating your beauty that it may instead help to bury it*. Statements of humility in those days were a form of flattery to persons of elevated station—particularly to potential patrons.

Flattery through exaggeration continues from there. He sets before himself the clearly impossible task of conveying in words the quality of that which can be appreciated only visually: "the beauty of your eyes." Then he says that even if he were to set down in fresh numbers (perhaps numbers of lines) the qualities that can be expressed in writing, his efforts would be futile. *So wonderful and fantastic are your qualities (your graces) that anyone who has to rely on appreciating you in the future by reading what I have written today would surely conclude that I am lying.*

The last line of the second quatrain is an outstanding display of Shakespeare's mastery of words. He juxtaposes the terms "heavenly" and "earthly" while using the term "touch" first as a noun and then as a verb.

Such heavenly touches ne'er touched earthly faces.

The beauty of that line is only part of its allure. With it, he implies that the sonnet's recipient exceeds typical human characteristics to such an extent as to suggest a parallel with that which might be found in heaven itself.

Continuing to conjecture about the reaction of future generations to his writing, he becomes graphic. He projects that his current writings will be seen in the future only as old yellowed paper, and himself as a liar—or at least a person prone to unjustifiable exaggeration. He sees himself becoming perceived as a hardcopy version of old men who sit around and spin wild tales. And that, he says, would rob the young man about whom he is writing of his true rights. Rather than being seen as Shakespeare recorded him, he would be regaled as the subject of a poet's irrational rantings—the "stretched meter of an antique song" (poetry and music were thought of as closely related in those times). All this self-flagellation is setting the table for the procreation message.

The couplet of Sonnet 15 (p. 124), as you will recall, promised to help keep the young man's beauty alive through verse, but that was only half the message. Sonnet 16 (not included in this book) completed it with advice to the young man to perpetuate his beauty by having a child. Shakespeare combines the same two messages within one sonnet here. After spending all three quatrains noting the futility of his verse, in the couplet he says:

But were some child of yours alive that time,
You should live twice—in it and in my rime.

My humble verse may yet help preserve your beauty if you give it credibility by having a child who can corroborate in the flesh what I say with my pen. Thus ends Shakespeare's series of procreation sonnets.

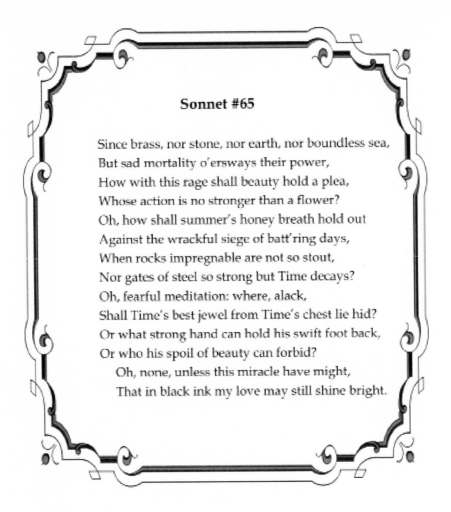

Sonnet #65

Since brass, nor stone, nor earth, nor boundless sea,
But sad mortality o'ersways their power,
How with this rage shall beauty hold a plea,
Whose action is no stronger than a flower?
Oh, how shall summer's honey breath hold out
Against the wrackful siege of batt'ring days,
When rocks impregnable are not so stout,
Nor gates of steel so strong but Time decays?
Oh, fearful meditation: where, alack,
Shall Time's best jewel from Time's chest lie hid?
Or what strong hand can hold his swift foot back,
Or who his spoil of beauty can forbid?
    Oh, none, unless this miracle have might,
    That in black ink my love may still shine bright.

The Essence of Sonnet #65

Time ravages all things, even the very powerful,
so what are the chances that beauty—fragile as it is—
can survive? Aha, perhaps it can survive in my verse.

To fully experience the sonnets visit www.sonnetsofshakespeare.com for a live recording by Darrel Walters.

Diagram for Greater Understanding

1st Quatrain

Since brass, nor stone, nor earth, nor boundless sea,

eventually Time topples them
But [sad mortality o'ersways their power,]

out-of-control carnage   defend itself
How with this [rage] shall beauty [hold a plea,]

force
Whose [action] is no stronger than a flower?

2nd Quatrain

sweetness
Oh, how shall summer's [honey breath] hold out

destructive attack
Against the [wrackful siege] of batt'ring days,

hardy
When rocks impregnable are not so [stout,]

Nor gates of steel so strong but Time decays?

3rd Quatrain

unfortunately
Oh, fearful meditation: where, [alack,]

beauty
Shall [Time's best jewel] from Time's chest lie hid?

Time's
Or what strong hand can hold [his] swift foot back,

Or who his spoil of beauty can forbid?

Couplet

idea has the needed strength
Oh, none, unless this [miracle have might,]

my writing
That in [black ink] my love may still shine bright.

SONNET 65

Description and Interpretation

The willful and notorious Mr. Time is a prominent actor in this sonnet. Brass, stone, earth, and sea: the people of late sixteenth-century England would surely have seen strength and long-term resilience in those objects. And yet Shakespeare notes that even their power is diminished by the unrelenting march of Time. Even they suffer a form of mortality. In the first two lines, he sets the stage for what he appropriately labels a "siege."

The softer elements of life, he says—chief among them being beauty—are infinitely less able than brass and stone to resist the destructive force of Time. What, then, are we to do to protect all that is beautiful against the assault of that old, familiar enemy?

In the second quatrain, he lays out still more symbols of strength torn asunder by Time: rocks and steel bars. This four-line segment is a rich repository of metaphors, imagery, and power—but it is more than that. It is a showcase of Shakespeare's skill in the use of word-sounds. The soft, smooth feeling of the vowel-dominated first line, representing beauty, gives way to the hard, jagged feeling of the consonant-dominated lines that follow.

> Oh, how shall summer's honey breath hold out
> Against the wrackful siege of batt'ring days,
> When rocks impregnable are not so stout.

The "wrackful siege" and the "batt'ring days" are not simply seen and heard: they are felt—their sharp edges cutting into nerve endings.

Time is depicted as the owner and holder of all that is. Metaphorically, he has an enormous chest in which he holds all of his possessions—that is, everyone and everything—and he has full control of them. He is the villain, the force to which all must eventually succumb, and Shakespeare worries aloud that the first to be trampled will be the weakest. He pictures Time's chest as a jewel chest, beauty being the most valuable of all the jewels it contains. And yet, because Time assaults everything in the chest, fragile beauty needs a place to hide or some form of protection.

Shakespeare's reverence for beauty shines brightly as the driving force behind his writing. His extreme sensitivity to the dangers that abound prompts him to open the third quatrain with "Oh, fearful meditation." *To even think about the impending carnage causes me to shake with fear.* C. L. Barber may have had such passages in mind when he wrote, in "The Sonnet as an Action,"

> The world is full of value that can be looked at front-face. Shakespeare could get more of this gold into his poetry than anyone else in the golden age because he had the greatest power of admiration. (1964, 160)

"Power of admiration." What a fine way that is to describe Shakespeare's observation of, sensitivity to, and regard for all that surrounded him!

Looking for a solution, Shakespeare asks "Where, alack, shall Time's best jewel from Time's chest lie hid?" Immediately, the fact that there is no place to hide becomes apparent to him. So he asks an equally unanswerable, rhetorical question:

> What strong hand can hold his swift foot back?

The futility is built into the question. Everyone knows instinctively that the force of a foot is too great to be held back by the weaker force of a hand.

The third and final rhetorical question of the third quatrain—"Who his spoil of beauty can forbid?"—is no more easily answered. He has built a strong case throughout the sonnet that the destruction of all by the villain Time is absolutely unstoppable. Brass, stone, earth, sea, rocks, steel bars—how will something "no stronger than a flower" be saved from a force with the power to overcome all those pillars of strength? In the couplet, after twelve lines of gloom and doom, he pulls a rabbit out of the hat. He writes as if preserving beauty in ink had just occurred to him, though he had by this time offered that solution several times previously. "Who his spoil of beauty can forbid?"

> Oh, none, unless this miracle have might,
> That in black ink my love may still shine bright.

How delightful the wordplay between "black" and "shine bright!"

After the first seventeen of Shakespeare's sonnets, the procreation sonnets, he abandoned the argument that the young man should have a child to preserve his beauty. His prescription for overcoming Time became the preservation of beauty through writing, as seen here. The most well-known of the sonnets carrying that theme, Sonnet 18, will complete this book.

Sonnet #18

Shall I compare thee to a summer's day?
Thou art more lovely and more temperate:
Rough winds do shake the darling buds of May,
And summer's lease hath all too short a date.
Sometime too hot the eye of heaven shines,
And often is his gold complexion dimmed;
And every fair from fair sometimes declines,
By chance, or Nature's changing course untrimmed;
But thy eternal summer shall not fade,
Nor lose possession of that fair thou owest,
Nor shall Death brag thou wand'rest in his shade,
When in eternal lines to Time thou growest.
  So long as men can breathe or eyes can see,
  So long lives this, and this gives life to thee.

The Essence of Sonnet #18

Most loveliness has its limitations, and in time
fades, but not so for yours. Your loveliness will
live eternally through this writing.

To fully experience the sonnets visit www.sonnetsofshakespeare.com for a
live recording by Darrel Walters.

Diagram for Greater Understanding

Shall I compare thee to a summer's day?

pleasant
Thou art more lovely and more [temperate:]

early summer is windy
[Rough winds do shake the darling buds of May,]

time in residence   **duration**
And summer's [lease] hath all too short a [date.]

sun
Sometime too hot the [eye of heaven] shines,

the weather overcast
And often is [his gold complexion dimmed;]

everything lovely
And [every fair] from fair sometimes declines,

unadjusted (nautical reference)
By chance or Nature's changing course [untrimmed;]

everlasting loveliness
But thy [eternal summer] shall not fade,

current loveliness
Nor lose possession of that [fair thou owest,]

that he's putting you in darkness
Nor shall Death brag [thou wand'rest in his shade,]

your path to life's end
When in [eternal lines to Time] thou growest.

people are here to read
So long as [men can breathe or eyes can see,]

my writing
So long lives [this,] and this gives life to thee.

SONNET 18

Description and Interpretation

A person who knows only one line from all of Shakespeare's sonnets probably knows the opening line of Sonnet 18: "Shall I compare thee to a summer's day?" Helen Vendler characterizes this sonnet as "the most familiar of the poems and the most indisputably Shakespearean" (1997, 120).

The ultimate message of Sonnet 18, *your loveliness will never fade*, sounds like a fantasy. It also sounds like a sentiment between a man and a woman. Scholars are quite sure it was written to the same young nobleman as many other sonnets. Still, many readers enjoy it as generic art, with a man/woman relationship in mind. There is no reason not to.

The sentiment of undying loveliness is powerful. We all think about how temporary life is and how time eventually will march on without us. We think of people from centuries past who had hopes and dreams and loves similar to ours—people whose bodies now lie moldering underground—and we shudder at the thought of where we and our loved ones are headed. We may find some comfort in this sonnet just knowing that Shakespeare thought profoundly about an issue that we think about.

Shakespeare spends the first two quatrains depicting the loveliness he wants to preserve, the loveliness of the sonnet's recipient. He does that by comparing it to a universally recognized loveliness: the loveliness of a summer's day. No sooner does he introduce his standard for beauty than he begins to point out its blemishes so as to elevate the beauty of the sonnet's recipient by comparison: the early part of summer is blustery, the best days of summer depart all too soon, and all of summer is unpredictable—sometimes too hot and sometimes overcast. His conclusion in these first two quatrains is that we cannot depend on loveliness to be constant. Then as we read on, we find we have been set up!

In the third quatrain, Shakespeare turns optimistic. He claims strongly that the specific loveliness he's writing about—the loveliness of this sonnet's recipient—is an exception to the temporariness he has attributed to loveliness in general. *Your loveliness*, he says, *will never fade*. He ties masterfully into his opening analogy by referring to "thy eternal summer" rather than to a less-imaginative *thy eternal loveli-*

ness. That is the kind of verbal sleight of hand we have come to expect from this master of language.

Because Shakespeare has hidden—all the way to the couplet—the premise that loveliness can be preserved in words, readers are led to see throughout the third quatrain that the man is most certainly walking onto a limb that will not support him. Is he actually saying, *you will never lose the loveliness you have now*? This can't be. We've all seen what advancing years do to youthful beauty. And most audacious is his claim that even death offers no threat to loveliness. We all know better!

Of course Shakespeare has deliberately positioned us to see his argument as unsupportable—even absurd. By doing so, he endows his punch line with more punch than it otherwise would have had. The ace he has up his sleeve is that loveliness resides in two dimensions. Loveliness within the physical dimension is temporary, but loveliness within the literary dimension is constant as long as the paper survives and someone is present to read it.

> So long as men can breathe or eyes can see,
> So long lives this, and this gives life to thee.

The words I've written here—describing your loveliness and claiming that it will last forever—in fact will cause it to last forever.

Of course one might try to debunk the spell of Sonnet 18 by using a little logic. Shakespeare hasn't given the summer's day a level playing field. The loveliness of the summer's day could live eternally as well if only he chose to put its loveliness into verse, as many great poets have.

But then logic and level playing fields are the province of scientists and lawyers. As an artist and a poet, Shakespeare uses his license to exercise romance over logic. And what he does with that license is startlingly effective. He has by implication parceled the universe into three entities: himself, the recipient of the sonnet, and everything else. He is saying to the recipient, *of all that exists in this universe, I have chosen to honor you alone with the preserving power of my eternal words.* That show of single-minded devotion gives Sonnet 18 a power that no amount of logic could match.

References

Auden, W. H. 2000. *Lectures on Shakespeare*, edited by Arthur Kirsch. Princeton, NJ: Princeton University Press.

Barber, C. L. 1964. "The Sonnet as an Action." In *Discussions of Shakespeare's Sonnets*, edited by Barbara Herrnstein, 159–64. Boston: C. C. Heath and Company.

———. 1987. "An Essay on Shakespeare's Sonnets." In *Modern Critical Interpretations: Shakespeare's Sonnets,* edited by Harold Bloom, 5–27. Philadelphia: Chelsea House Publishers.

Blackmur, R. P. 1962. "A Poetics for Infatuation." In *The Complete Sonnets: Interpretive Essays*, edited by Blackmur, R. P., Leslie A. Fiedler, Northrop Frye, Edward Hubler, Stephen Spender, and Oscar Wilde, 131–61. New York: Basic Books, Inc.

Booth, Stephen. 2000, 1977. *Shakespeare's Sonnets, Edited with Analytic Commentary*. New Haven, CT: Yale University Press.

Cruttwell, Patrick. 1964. "Shakespeare's Sonnets and the 1590s." In *Discussions of Shakespeare's Sonnets*, edited by Barbara Herrnstein, 46–55. Boston: C. C. Heath and Company.

Frye, Northrop. 1962. "How True a Twain." In *The Complete Sonnets: Interpretive Essays*, edited by Blackmur, R. P., Leslie A. Fiedler, Northrop Frye, Edward Hubler, Stephen Spender, and Oscar Wilde, 25–53. New York: Basic Books, Inc.

Giroux, Robert. 1982. *The Book Known as Q: A Consideration of Shakespeare's Sonnets*. New York: Antheneum

Hubler, Edward. 1952. *The Sense of Shakespeare's Sonnets.* New York: Hill and Wang.

———. 1962. "Shakespeare's Sonnets and the Commentators." In *The Complete Sonnets: Interpretive Essays*, edited by Blackmur, R. P., Leslie A.

Fiedler, Northrop Frye, Edward Hubler, Stephen Spender, and Oscar Wilde, 3–21. New York: Basic Books, Inc.

Jones, Katherine Duncan, ed. 1997. *Shakespeare's Sonnets*. From the Arden Shakespeare Series. London: Thomas Nelson and Sons Ltd. ‡

Kay, Dennis. 1998. *William Shakespeare: Sonnets and Poems*. From the *Twayne English Authors Series*, edited by Arthur G. Kinney. New York: Twayne Publishers, an Imprint of Simon & Schuster Macmillan.

Lederer, Richard. 1991. *The Miracle of Language*. New York: Pocket Books, a division of Simon and Schuster Inc.

Lever, J. W. 1956. *The Elizabethan Love Sonnet*. London: Methuen & Co. Ltd.

Schoenfeldt, Michael. 2010. *The Cambridge Introduction to Shakespeare's Poetry*. Cambridge, UK: Cambridge University Press.

Smith, Hallet. 1952. *Elizabethan Poetry: A Study in Conventions, Meaning, and Expression*. Cambridge, MA: Harvard University Press.

Vendler, Helen. 1997. *The Art of Shakespeare's Sonnets*. Cambridge, MA: The Belknap Press of Harvard University Press.

Willen, Gerald, and Victor B. Reed, eds. 1964. *A Casebook on Shakespeare's Sonnets*. New York: Thomas Y. Crowell Company.‡

Wright, Louis B., ed. 1967. *Shakespeare's Sonnets,* The Folger Library General Reader's Shakespeare. New York: Simon & Schuster, Inc.*

---

*This volume of *The Sonnets* is the source for sonnets as presented in *The Wit and Wisdom of Shakespeare*, with minor alterations as follows.

A few alternate punctuation marks have been chosen here—in keeping primarily with other editions, and occasionally with the author's preference. Most notable are the exclamation points in Sonnet 37 at the end of the last line, in Sonnet 43 at the ends of lines eight and twelve, and in Sonnet 115 at the end of line eight. The practice of applying exclamation points as they are used today to *The Sonnets* is mixed among the various editions. This author prefers to avoid them.

In Sonnet 2, line four, the term *tottered*—meaning *ragged*—in some editions has been emended to *tattered*. This author has chosen to use that emendation.

In Sonnet 37, some editions read "entitled in *thy* parts" and others "entitled in *their* parts," with interpretive arguments available for both. This author has chosen to use *their*, the term used by Shakespeare in the 1609 edition.

In Sonnets 116 and 55, this author has chosen to leave the terms *doom* and *judgment* in lower case, as they are in the 1609 edition.

In sonnet 80, line eleven, the term *wracked* is emended to *wrecked* in some editions. This author has chosen to use that emendation.

‡ Explanatory notes from these volumes were consulted for some sonnets to help seed the author's thinking as he prepared the diagrams.

Index

References are to narrative pages only, with sonnet content described briefly in the Table of Contents and elaborated upon in diagrams.